IF 12|05

$8.51

Ancestry's

CONCISE
GENEALOGICAL
DICTIONARY

compiled by
Maurine and Glen Harris

P.O. Box 476
Salt Lake City, Utah 84110

Harris, Maurine, 1946-
        Ancestry's concise genealogical dictionary / compiled by
Maurine and Glen Harris
                p. cm.
        Bibliography
        ISBN 0-916489-06-X
        1. Genealogy—Dictionaries. I. Harris, Glen, 1943-.
II. Title.
CS6.H37 1989
929'.1'03—dc19   89-6502

Cover Design by Newman Passey Design, Inc.

First Printing 1989
10 9 8 7 6

Printed in the United States of America

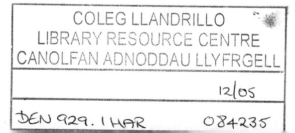

Contents

Preface

GENEALOGICAL RESEARCH, by its very nature, presents family historians with a stubborn and unavoidable problem: words encountered in original records are often dated or even obsolete; many terms are legal, medical, or governmental jargon; and there is a myriad of Latin terminology in probates, deeds, and church records. *Ancestry's Concise Genealogical Dictionary* is meant to be at least a partial solution to this problem. As it is inconvenient to haul all twelve volumes of the Oxford English Dictionary and a host of other such reference works on each trip to a library or a courthouse, we thought it would be appropriate for the family history researcher to have a concise, informative guide, a genealogist's dictionary, of common, and even not so common, terms encountered during genealogical research.

The words included in this guide may be found in apprentice, church, census, tax, land, naturalization, immigration, and medical records, as well as in deeds, probates, civil registrations, and poll books. The terms were collected over years of genealogical research from innumerable original records, as well as from other genealogical reference books, such as *The Source*. The definitions were compiled and verified using several dictionaries and encyclopedias, including the *Oxford English Dictionary, Black's Law Dictionary,* various foreign language dictionaries, and a nineteenth-century edition of Webster's, which helped greatly in determining precisely the meanings of dated terms at the time they were in use.

This is a concise, specialized dictionary. It is not meant to give all the meanings of any particular term but only those which are unusual or dated and that are most pertinent (considering the term was likely encountered in one or another of the sources listed above). For example, the definition of the word "perch" describes a unit of land measurement and does not include everyday meanings, such as "a roost for a bird," that may not be relevant to a genealogist's research. Thus, this book is meant to be compact and portable so that it can be carried to the site of research easily, and specialized so that one does not have to sort through a myriad of meanings to arrive at the one most likely implied in a genealogical or historical context.

For more thorough and comprehensive definitions, we encourage you to consult those works listed in the bibliography, from which the meanings listed in this work were gleaned. We are aware too, that there are many such terms that should be added to this compendium and we welcome contributions for future editions. It is our hope that this publication will aid researchers and make their work more productive and comprehensible, thus adding to the enjoyment and fulfillment of the family history search.

Multiple Definitions

When there are two or more definitions given for the same term, they will be numbered.

> **taille:** 1: a feudal tax imposed by a king or a lord. 2: the waist or bodice of a gown.

If the definitions are very closely related they will simply be separated by semicolons.

> **abavus:** (*Lat.*) second great-grandfather; ancestor.

Spelling Variations

It should be mentioned that spelling has not always been as standardized as it is today. For some time in English, *y* and *i* could be used interchangeably, for example. For this reason we have tried to include the most common variations of many words and utilized cross references to lead to the definition. However, it would be difficult, and much bulkier, to include all variations of all words. If you are unable to find a term, you will want to consider checking for it under variant spellings.

Cross References

A term that is synonymous with another, defined elsewhere in the dictionary, will have a cross reference to the defined term. At the base term, i.e., the one with the definition, there will be an "also" reference listing all the variations and synonyms of the term that are included in the dictionary.

Some terms that are not exactly synonymous, but which are related to other terms defined in the dictionary, will also have cross references following the main definition. These cross references will direct the reader to another entry which will elaborate on the topic in question.

Using this Dictionary

Guidewords

Guidewords are provided at the top of each page. The left-hand word indicates the first word that appears on the page and the right-hand word indicates the last word to appear on the page. The guidewords simply speed the process of looking up a term by allowing one to scan these words and quickly find the page on which the desired term appears.

The Entry

The term to be defined appears in boldface type and is followed by a colon. If the definition to follow is not in current English usage, then a statement in parenthesis indicates when and/or where the term was in use, if it is obsolete, archaic, slang, etc.

> **boumet:** (*obsolete*) to embalm.

If there are other terms which mean the same thing, a list of these synonyms appears in brackets as an "also" reference.

> **chemise:** [*also* shift] a woman's shirt-like undergarment.

Occasionally there will be further comment on or brief example of usage, in addition to the definition. This comment is separated from the main definition by an em-dash.

> **mulatto:** the offspring of one white and one black parent —sometimes used, especially on census schedules, for Indians.

A small number of entries have been quoted directly from sources such as the *Oxford English Dictionary*. In these cases the definition is given in quotes and the name of the source follows.

Bibliography

An American Dictionary of the English Language. Edited by Noah Webster. New York: S. Converse, 1828.

The American Heritage Dictionary of the English Language. Edited by William Morris. Boston: Houghton Mifflin Company, 1979.

Henry C. Black. *Black's Law Dictionary.* 4th ed. St. Paul, Minn.: West Publishing, 1951.

Leon L. Bram, Norma H. Dickey, and Robert S. Phillips. *Funk and Wagnalls New Encyclopedia.* R.R. Donnelley and Sons, 1983.

A Dictionary of American English. Edited by William A Craigie, and James R. Hulbert. Chicago: University of Chicago, 1940.

Arlene Eakle, and Johni Cerny, eds. *The Source: A Guidebook of American Genealogy.* Salt Lake City, Utah: Ancestry Publishing, 1984.

Steven H. Gifis. *Law Dictionary.* Woodbury, N.Y.: Barron's Educational Series, 1975.

Charles F. Hemphill, Jr., and Phyllis D. Hemphill. *Dictionary of Practical Law.* Englewood Cliffs, N.J.: Prentice-Hall, 1979.

The Oxford English Dictionary. Edited by Henry Bradley, W.A. Craigie, C.T. Onions, and James A.H. Murray. 12 vols. Reprint. Great Britain: Oxford University Press, 1961.

Webster's New 20th Century Dictionary. Edited by Jean L. McKechnie. 2nd ed. New York: Simon and Schuster, 1979.

A

Ab: in the Jewish calendar, the eleventh month of the civil year, or the fifth month of the ecclesiastical year (July and part of August); in the Syrian calendar, the twelfth or last summer month (August).

abatement: 1: the difference between the amount of the estate an heir is to receive as specified in a will and the amount actually received, due to property devaluation between the time the will was made and when the death occurred; the entry of a stranger into the estate after the death of the possessor but before the heir or devisee can take control. 2: in heraldry, a mark of dishonor in a coat of arms, the most common of which was the point and gore, which cut off an angle on the shield and was awarded for lying, boasting, drunkenness, killing a prisoner who had surrendered, rape, and sloth in war.

abavus: (*Lat.*) second great-grandfather; ancestor.

abbess: the female superior of a nunnery or convent.

abbey: religious house where monks or nuns live in seclusion from the world under vows of celibacy, poverty, or obedience.

abbot: [*also* abbod] the superior of an abbey or monastery for men.

abbreviate of adjudication: abstract of a court record showing the amount of land debts and the names of creditors and debtors.

abdominal typhus: a type of typhus fever characterized by bluish spots appearing on the abdomen a few days after the disease is contracted.

aberemord: (*Lat.*) murder fully proved, as distinguished from manslaughter and accidental death.

abesse: (*Lat.*) *literally* "to be off"; absence.

abeyance: the condition of an estate which either has been claimed but not taken possession of, or which is liable to be claimed by someone.

abeyd: (*England before the colonization of America; colonial New England*) abide.

ab initio: (*Lat.*) [*also* ab initus] *literally* "from the beginning"; used in reference to situations regarding the validity of a deed, marriage, estate, etc.

ab intestate: (*Lat.*) the condition of inheriting from one who died without making a will.

abjurer: one who renounces an oath, as an alien seeking naturalization who was required to renounce allegiance to his former country or government.

ablepsia: [*also* ablepsy] blindness.

abluent: a substance which thins, purifies, or sweetens the blood, commonly used in nineteenth-century England and colonial America.

ablution: washing the body externally or internally with diluting fluids.

ab nepos: (*Lat.*) great-great-grandson.

ab neptis: (*Lat.*) great-great-granddaughter.

abode: a place of habitual dwelling or residence.

abolitionist: a person supporting the immediate extinction of black slavery in the United States.

Abolition Society: organization formed to work for the elimination of slavery and involuntary servitude (1820-70s).

aborigine: an original, indigenous inhabitant of a country.

abortivus: (*Lat.*) born prematurely.

abracadabra: a cabalistic word, used as a charm, and believed to have the power to cure illness and disease when written in a triangular arrangement and worn around the neck.

Abraham Man: (*originally*) a lunatic member of Abraham Ward, Bethlehem Hospital, London, allowed to beg in the streets; (*sixteenth- and seventeenth-century England)* a vagabond beggar, usually feigning lunacy, who wandered the countryside, especially after the dissolution of the religious houses.

abruptio: (*Lat.*) *literally* "breaking off"; divorce, most often found in church records such as parish books and legal documents.

abscess (of liver): a collection of purulent matter or pockets of pus, usually fatal, sometimes caused by amebic dysentery.

absentee: A Loyalist who, supporting the British Crown, left his residence and lived elsewhere, usually out of the country, during the American Revolution.

absentee ballot: a ballot in American elections completed by a person absent from his usual voting precinct.

absolution record: a book or list kept by a minister containing the names of those requesting absolution from sin.

absque: (*Lat.*) without; but for.

abstract: to take the main points and essential information from a document such as a will, deed, bounty land warrant, census, etc.

abstract book: land record book containing information in condensed form which usually lists the names of land purchasers chronologically, and is kept in the district land offices or with the Bureau of Land Management.

abstracted medical record: a record prepared for soldiers treated at medical facilities in posts, camps, and in the field, containing name, rank, unit, reason for treatment, and treatment time period.

abstract of title: shortened version of all documents affecting the title to a certain piece of land including a listing of all actions, decrees, conveyances, and written instruments as well as all persons who had dealings with a particular property, thus giving all the necessary information concerning the title to the land.

abut: to adjoin or border such as in land, estates, or farms.

abuttal: a boundary where one's land joins or meets another's land.

Acadian: inhabitant of Acadia (Nova Scotia); a descendant of French settlers of Acadia who live in Louisiana, i.e., Cajuns.

acceptance: 1: a file of Naval Officers containing information such as age, name, birthplace, and place at the time of acceptance of the appointment which can be found in the Naval records in the National Archives. 2: a record of new converts or arrivals admitted into church fellowship.

accession number: number assigned by a librarian or archivist denoting the time a book, manuscript, or artifact was placed within a collection.

accipitrary: (*nineteenth-century English*) a falconer or keeper and tamer of hawks.

accommodation: land allotted to families in a town or settlement.

accommodation note: a statement, draft, or paper drawn for the purpose of obtaining credit with no consideration.

accompt: account.

accretion: the right of inheritance by survival.

acheat: *see* escheat.

aches: (*colonial American*) [*also* pricking aches] convulsions.

achete: *see* escheat.

achievement: a heraldic insignia which is the shield with all its adjuncts, of which the basic six are (1) the shield, sometimes called the "coat of arms," (2) the helmet, (3) the mantling or lambrequin, (4) the wreath or torse, (5) the crest, and (6) the motto.

achor: "the scald head, a disease forming scaly eruptions, supposed to be critical evacuation of acrimonious humors; a species of herpes."—*Webster's*

acme: the period of full growth or mature age, often used in medical records to describe the maturity of a person.

acolyte: the highest of the inferior orders of Roman Catholic clergy having the responsibility of assisting at the altar.

aconite: a medicine made from the dried root of the monkshood used to reduce fever, as a sedative, and as a painkiller.

acquired land: federal land acquired through purchase, because of condemnation, or as gifts, which is under the jurisdiction of the public land laws.

acre-dale: a common field in which several proprietors held interest, not necessarily on equal basis.

acre-man: (*Middle English*) a man who ploughed or cultivated the land.

acreme: (*obsolete*) a square acre or a piece of land a furlong square.

acre-shot: (*obsolete*) a tax or charge per acre. *See* acre-tax.

acre-tax: English method of taxing land at a certain amount per acre.

act: [*also* Pastoral Act; Ministerial Act] the sacramental acts of baptism, burial, confirmation, communion, etc.

Act Book: a record of the sacramental acts of baptism, burial, confirmation, marriage, communion, etc, performed by the minister in various denominations.

acton: a stuffed jacket made of quilted cotton and worn under a coat of mail; in later times, a jacket of leather or other material plated with mail.

actoures: (*obsolete*) manager, overseer, or agent.

actual grant: in colonial America, a grant made by the English Crown but which, in reality, could not be made by English law as the title of the land was subject to the right of occupancy.

acyce: (*obsolete*) assize.

Adamatine: 1: a hard wax candle. 2: a member of the extreme faction of the Hardshells, the New York Conservative Democratic political party.

Adamite: 1: a supporter of John Adams, second President of the United States (1797-1801) or of his son John Quincy Adams, sixth president (1825-29). 2: in pre-fifteenth-century Christian history, a religious sect wishing to establish a state of innocence that went naked (like Adam) and barred marriage as a sin.

ad collingendum: (*Lat.*) an administrator or trustee appointed to hold an estate until an administrator or trustee with the proper power is appointed by the court.

adde: (*Lat.*) add.

addice: (*obsolete*) adz; an axe-like tool.

Addison File: (1848-62) a file created by a clerk in the Officers and Enlisted Men's Department which was transferred to the Enlisted Branch in 1862, concerning the military service of enlisted men.

addition: a title or name added to a man's christian or surname, to show his rank, occupation, or residence.

additur: (*Lat.*) *literally* "let there be added"; the increase in the amount of money awarded by the judge over the amount decided on by the jury because he considered it an unjust award.

Address Book: (1860-94) a three volume set identifying surgeons and assistant surgeons in volunteer organizations in the United States Army.

ademption: a removal or a taking away; in law, a situation when a specific legacy in a will was not carried out or bequeathed because it was no longer in the possession of the testator at the time of death.

ad exhaeredationem: (*Lat.*) to disinherit.

adfiliation: (*obsolete*) affiliation. *See* adoption by matrimony.

ad hoc: (*Lat.*) for this special reason; for a special purpose.

ad interim: (*Lat.*) meanwhile, temporary, as an appointment made for a temporary time or as a fill-in.

adjacent proprietor: a person who owns a bordering or adjoining piece of property.

Adjutant General: on both the federal and state level, the highest administrative position or office in the army.

ad locum: (*Lat.*) to or at the place.

admeasure: to give each heir or claimant his or her rightful share of an estate, dower, or property.

admeasurement: the adjustment or apportionment of the shares of an estate, dower, pasture held in common, inheritance, etc.

admeasurement of dower: the readjustment of a dower when an heir becomes of age because a parent or guardian was receiving an unfair share to support the child.

administration: the management or settling of the estate of a person who died without a will, of a person whose estate is being handled by an executor under a will, or of a minor or mentally incompetent person.

administration bond: a specified amount of money, usually twice the estimated value of the estate, posted by the person chosen by the court to act as administrator of an estate which insures that the administrator will fulfill his obligations satisfactorily according to law.

administration cum testamento annexo: *see* administration with will annexed.

administration de bonis non: administration of a deceased person's property that was not completely distributed by the first administrator.

administration de bonis non cum testamento annexo: administration granted by the court when part of the estate is still unadministered because of the death of the executor.

administration of estates: court supervised management, settlement, and distribution of an estate by an administrator or

executor whose duties usually involve collection and payment of debts, and distribution of the remainder of the estate.

administration pendite lite: administration of an estate carried out while a suit is pending concerning the validity of the will.

administration with will annexed: [*also* administration cum testamento annexo] administration granted by the court in instances where the person who makes a will has neglected to name an executor, or where the executor is unable or refuses to act.

administrator: a person appointed by the court to administer the estate of an incompetent person or an intestate who differs from an executor in that he is court appointed whereas the executor is appointed by the deceased.

administrator cum testamento annexo: *see* administrator with will annexed.

administrator de bonis non: *literally* "of the goods not administered"; the portion of an estate which is granted to the administration of a person who has been appointed to succeed

7

a previous administrator, who has left the estate partially unsettled.

administrator deed: [*also* executor deed] a document given to the purchaser as a result of a sale conducted by the administrator in behalf of the estate including the sale of real property, cattle, slaves, household goods, etc., and is usually indexed in the name of the administrator.

administrator with will annexed: [*also* administrator cum testamento annexo] a person granted administration in cases where a testator makes a will without naming any executors, where the executors who are named in the will are incompetent to act or refuse to act, and in the event of the death of the executors.

administratrix: a female administrator.

admiralty court: [*also* American Court of Vice Admiralty; Court of the Lord High Admiral; Court of the Admiral; High Court of Admiralty; English High Court of Admiralty; High Court of Admiralty in England] an organization having jurisdiction in cases having to do with admiralty law, anything to do with the seas, and also with navigable rivers, which originally handled only cases of piracy and spoils, but eventually gained jurisdiction over all maritime matters.

admiralty droit: a jurisdiction of the admiralty court which handles cases involving the right of one nation to capture property belonging to another.

admission: [*also* Admission to Citizenship; Orders of Admission to Citizenship] naturalization; the court order, a part of the naturalization process, admitting the person to citizenship who had successfully met the requirements for becoming a citizen.

admittatur: a certificate of admission signed by a principal administrator, usually of a college, for a particular student.

Admitted Cherokee Freedman: Cherokee freedman records.

admitted freeman: *see* indentured servant.

Adoptees' Liberty Movement Association: an organization that helps individuals find their natural families having regional branches and maintaining a registry for adoptees and parents (Adoptees Liberty Movement Association, P.O. Box 154, Washington Bridge Station, New York, NY 10033).

adoption by arms: a pre-1600 ceremony of presenting arms to a person based on merit or valor, who was then under an obligation to defend the giver.

adoption by baptism: a spiritual affinity contracted between godfathers and godchildren in the baptism ceremony, and entitled the godchild to a share of the godfather's estate.

adoption by hair: a ceremony performed to indicate adoption by cutting off a piece of hair and giving it to the adoptive father.

adoption by matrimony: the act of taking the children of a spouse's former marriage as one's own upon marriage.

adoption by testament: to appoint a person heir if he follows the stipulations in the will to take the name, arms, etc., of the adopter.

adorat: (*archaic*) a chemical weight of four pounds.

adulterine: (*nineteenth century*) a child born of an adulterous relationship.

ad valorem tax: (*Lat.*) *literally* "according to value"; a tax which is imposed according to the value of the property, and differs from a specific duty or tax which is put on each article regardless of value.

advancement: a gift given to a child by a living parent in anticipation of an inheritance.

Advent: a moveable feast day, Advent Sunday is the Sunday nearest 30 November (i.e., nearest the Feast of St. Andrew and four Sundays before Christmas).

Advent Christian Church: a church which acquired the name Advent Christian Church in 1861, whose members, better known as Adventists or Seventh-Day Adventists, believe the second coming (Advent) of Christ and the end of the world are close at hand.

adventurer: one who purchased shares in the Virginia Land Company, at 12 pounds 10 shillings each, and received 100 acres in Virginia. *See* Virginia Company of London.

ad verbatim: (*Lat.*) *literally "to the word"*; in full.

adverse possession: actual possession of real property obtained by aggressive or "notorious" actions, and gaining title to the property by keeping it for a statutory period of time.

advowtery: (*obsolete: fifteenth-seventeenth century*) adultery.

adz: a carpenter's or cooper's tool resembling an ax with the blade set at right angles to the handle and curving inward towards it.

aet: (*obsolete*) food.

aetas: (*Lat.*) lifetime; age; generation.

aetatis: (*Lat.*) of age or aged.

aetatis suae: (*Lat.*) the condition of being in a specified year of one's life—aetatis suae 25 means in the twenty-fifth year of one's age, after a person's twenty-fourth birthday.

aetatula: (*Lat.*) very tender childhood, indicates a very young child.

affeeror: a manorial court officer who assessed the penalty or restitution due from an offender.

affiance: betrothal.

affidavit: a written document created while under oath before an authorized officer such as a notary public, court officer, etc.

affinage: a refining of metal.

affinity: one's relationship to the spouse's relatives as opposed to the blood relationship of one's own relatives.

affirmation: a declaration made by a person having conscientious objections against swearing an oath.

affusion: water poured upon the body, often as a method of baptism.

African Consumption: (*slang*) consumption (tuberculosis) suffered by a Negro, usually a slave.

African Methodist Episcopal Church: a church founded by black parishioners of the Methodist Church in 1816 in Philadelphia dissatisfied with religious prejudice after a movement actually begun in 1787 under the leadership of the church's first bishop, Richard

Allen, an itinerant preacher and former slave.

African Methodist Episcopal Zion Church: a church founded by black parishioners of the Methodist Episcopal Church in 1796 in New York dissatisfied with their small role in leadership in the churches. James Varick became the first bishop in 1821, and in 1848 it adopted the current name.

after-acquired property: property that was acquired after the date of a will.

after kindred: (*pre-nineteenth century*) remote relatives.

age of consent: age at which persons can marry without parental consent.

age of contractibility: age below which legal marriages could not be contracted, with or without parental consent.

age of discretion: age at which persons can choose their own guardians.

age of majority: age at which a person becomes able to handle his own affairs being usually 18 for girls and 21 for boys.

age of reason: age at which a child is considered capable of acting responsibly, being commonly age seven or eight.

aggregate (census): an enumeration in which no names are recorded, only the number of individuals within an age group, religious group, type of profession, national origin, etc.

aght: (*obsolete*) possessions; property.

aghtand: (*obsolete*) eighth.

agistment: the keeping and feeding of cattle or livestock at a rate per head; the opening of a forest or meadow for a specified period of time to livestock.

agistment tithe: the tithe of cattle or other produce of grasslands paid to a vicar or rector.

aglutition: inability to swallow, frequently found on death certificates.

agnate: (*Lat.*) a kinsman who is traceable exclusively through males, on the father's side; descendants by male links from the same male ancestor.

agnati: (*Lat.*) relatives on the father's side.

agrarian: a person who favors an equal division of landed property, or a change in the ownership of the land.

ague: originally the feverish stage, but afterwards more usually the cold or shivering stage of an acute or violent fever; a malarial fever.

ague-cake: a hard tumor or swelling on the left side of the abdomen, lower than the false rib, resulting from enlargement of the spleen or liver, and supposed to be the effect of intermitting fevers.

ague tree: sassafras, a tree effective in reducing fevers.

aid: a payment from a tenant to his lord, abolished in 1660, which was made in the instance of the eldest daughter's marriage, the eldest son's knighthood, or to pay ransom.

aik: (*obsolete*) oak.

ais: *see* alias.

ait: [*also* eyot] an islet or small isle—an ait or eyot of the Thames River, for example.

aker: (*obsolete*) acre.

aksis: (*obsolete*) access, an intense feeling of fever or ague.

Alabama Claims: (1872) claims for losses to Confederate privateer ships such as the Alabama, the Shenandoah, the Florida, and the Tallahassee, described in Department of State publication, *Revised List of Claims Filed with the Department of State, Growing out of the Acts Committed by the Several Vessels, Which Have Given Rise to the Claims Generically Known as the Alabama Claims.*

alamode: a plain, soft, lustrous silk used in the eighteenth century for making hoods, mantuas, and for lining various garments.

albumen print: paper developed by L.D. Blanquart-Evard which was used for photographs from 1851 to 1895 and was extremely thin and smooth with high gloss and a sepia-brown color.

alcalde: 1: old miner's courts established in the 1800s in the Old West which dispensed justice in areas where there were no local or county governments. 2: a Spanish magistrate or mayor.

alderman: the governor of a district; the chief executive officer of a guild; a municipal officer.

ale: a country festival in which ale was the predominate drink.

aleberry: [*also* alebrue; alemeat] a beverage used in England in the 1800s of ale boiled with spice and sugar and bits of bread, sometimes used for invalids.

aleconner: a London officer in the eighteenth and nineteenth centuries who inspected the measures used in public houses to prevent fraud in selling liquors.

ale-draper: (*obsolete*) an alehouse keeper.

alemeat: *see* aleberry.

ale-taster: an English officer appointed in every court leet, and sworn to inspect ale, beer, and bread, and examine the quality and quantity within his precincts.

alewife: 1: a woman who keeps an alehouse. 2: an American fish first used by the Indians and then by the Colonists as fertilizer.

Algonkin Indians: [*also* Algonquin] an American Indian tribe which inhabited eastern and Midwestern states and parts of Canada.

alguaz: a sheriff or law enforcement officer in regions under Spanish influence.

Al-Hal-Day: (*archaic*) *All* Hallows Day or All Saints Day.

alias: [*also* alius; ais] an assumed name.

alias dictus: *literally* "otherwise called."

aliases: otherwise, at another time, formerly called—used to link the names of a man and wife if she was the last of her line and wished to perpetuate her family name.

alien: 1: [*also* aliene] in land transactions, the transfer of property which has unrestricted ownership. 2: a person born in another country who has no legal rights. 3: a class of citizenship in the colonies which pertained to those born outside the British Empire and not entitled to the rights of an Englishman.

Alien and Sedition Acts: acts restricting aliens during wartime which, beginning in 1798, defined all male citizens of a nation formally at war with the United States age 14 or older as alien enemies and applied in 1812 to all British subjects required to report to U.S. marshals.

alienate: to transfer clear title to property.

alienation: the right to transfer title and possession of property to another.

alien declaration: declarations in the form of affidavits, oaths, or other written notices of an alien's intention to become a citizen.

Alien Draft Files: federal records (1862-64) relating to aliens drafted into the United States Army and released including documents such as depositions, draft notices, and correspondence about releases.

alien letters: federal records (1812-14) written by U.S. Marshals relating to enemy aliens.

alien manifest: early 1900 records which show aliens employed as crew members on a ship.

alien prisoner of war lists: federal records (1812-15) of prisoners delivered to U.S. Marshals from U.S. ships.

alien re-entry permit: a permit issued to an alien allowing visits abroad for up to two years followed by the privilege of re-entry into the country.

alien registration: the process of keeping track of aliens by requiring that they register and carry proof of their registration.

alien registration receipt card: the card an alien was required to carry according to the requirements of a 1940 act.

alien returns: federal records (1812-15) which were reports by U.S. Marshals about all British subjects to the Department of State.

alien sailing authorization lists: federal records (1812-15) which included people authorized to sail from the United States during the War of 1812, created primarily at the port of Philadelphia.

aliene: to transfer property or title to another. *See* alien.

alienee: the buyer, or the person to whom the ownership of property is transferred.

alienus: (*Lat.*) 1: another's. 2: foreign. 3: hostile.

alii: (*Lat.*) others.

aliquot part: a public domain land measurement meaning a quarter division of a section of ground, generally a division into equal parts.

alius: *see* alias.

allegation: application for license to marry.

allen: a field or open land ploughed and left to grow weeds to be used as pasture land.

alleys of the house: a passage between the rows of pews or seats in a church; church aisles.

All-Hallows: All Saints Day, the first of November.

allodial title: owned freely without obligation or restriction.

allottery: the action of allotting or assignment of a share.

almesse: (*obsolete*) alms.

almoner: an officer who distributes charity or alms—by ancient law every monastery was to disperse a tenth of its income in alms to the poor, and all bishops were obliged to keep an almoner.

alms: charitable gifts given to the poor.

almshouse: workhouse; a house founded by private charity for the care of the poor.

almsman: (*Victorian England*) a person supported by charity or one who lived on alms.

alnager: a sworn officer appointed to examine and measure woolen cloth and fix a seal upon it if it passed inspection.

alner: 1: almoner. 2: (*obsolete*) purse. 3: (*obsolete: rare*) to measure by the ell.

alumnus: (*Lat.*) foster son.

alure: a walk or passage behind the parapets of a castle, or around the roof over a church by a covered passage.

alutation: (*obsolete*) a tanning of leather.

amalgamation: (*colonial American*) the fusion of the white and black races by intermarriage.

amalgamationist: one who favors the union of the black and white races.

Amana Church Society: [*also* Ebenezer Society] an organization founded in Germany, in 1842, which settled near Buffalo and organized the Ebenezer Society in 1843 and, in 1855, removing to Iowa County, Iowa, and in 1859 became the Amana Society.

ambrotype: a photographic process developed by Frederick Arches and Peter Fry in England, developed 1855 to 1870, which displays the image on glass, usually backed with black material.

ambry: a storehouse, cupboard, repository, or any place used for storage.

ambulatory: a passageway running around the back of the altar of a church.

amendment: 1: (*obsolete*) improvement of soil by using manure or compost. 2: a document issued to change something in a previously issued document.

a mensa et thoro: *literally* "from table and bed," but commonly "from bed and board"; a legal separation rather than a divorce.

amentia: feeblemindedness; a temporary, confused state of insanity.

amerce: to give a penalty (amercement) of money for an offence in the manorial court.

American Courts of Vice Admiralty: *see* admiralty court.

American Party: a political party active in national affairs from 1853 to 1859 which was antagonistic to the influence of foreign-born persons or ideas and was called the Know-nothing Party.

American plague: yellow fever.

American State Papers: a compilation of the most important legislation and executive documents created by the United States and as selected by the Secretary of the Senate and Clerk of the House of Representatives, 1789 to 1838. The first edition of thirty-eight volumes was arranged as follows: category 1 (6 volumes), Foreign Relations; category 2 (2 volumes), Indian Affairs; category 3 (5 volumes), Finance; category 4 (2 volumes), Commerce and Navigation; category 5 (7 volumes), Military Affairs; category 6 (4 volumes), Naval Affairs; category 7 (1 volume), Post-Office Department; category 8 (8 volumes), Public Lands (meaning the disposal of public land by the federal government); category 9 (1 volume), Claims (meaning private land claims by individuals). Each volume is indexed individually and a computerized index to the nine volumes in categories eight and nine is *Grassroots of Americana Computerized Index to the American State Papers: Land Grants and Claims (1789-1837)*, Salt Lake City: Gendex Corporation, 1972.

amice: cloth used for a loose wrap; an oblong piece of white linen, originally enveloping the head and neck, folded to lie around the neck and shoulders; part of the clothing of the religious orders.

amicus: (*Lat.*) friend, ally.

amicus curiae: *literally* "friend of the court"; an attorney or a layman, called in to advise the court on some legal matter.

Amish: a member of a Mennonite group begun by Jacob Ammann (Amen) in the 1600s.

amita: (*Lat.*) father's sister (aunt).

amita magna: (*Lat.*) grandfather's sister; grand aunt.

amnesty files: direct applications to the president (1865-67) which include applications, oaths of allegiance, and supporting documents of southerners who had held high civilian or military rank, or who owned property valued at $20,000 or more.

amnesty oath files: (1863-66) files including the oath, acknowledgment of warrants of presidential pardons, and an agreement to accept conditions of pardon.

amnesty pardons: (1865-67) lists of persons accepting amnesty pardons and copies of presidential pardons.

Anabaptist: [*also* catabaptist] name given to Swiss Mennonites and others who believed only in adult baptism as being scriptural, and refusing to allow their infants to be baptized.

Groups developing from the Anabaptist movement were Mennonites, Huterites, Adventists, Pennsylvania Germans, and the Baptists.

anaplerotic: a medicine which promotes the healing process, and helps renew flesh or wasted parts—often found in medical records.

anascara: a form of dropsy where there is swelling just beneath the skin which produces a very puffed appearance of the flesh over a large surface of the body.

ancessoure: (*obsolete*) ancestor.

Ancestral File: a computerized file created by the Family History Department of the LDS Church in which are entered family groups and lineage linked (parent to child in a repetitive process) records, tracing backward in time to common ancestry.

ancestress: a female ancestor.

ancient: ensign; a standard bearer or ancient bearer.

Ancient and Honorable Artillery Company of Massachusetts: [*also* the Military Company of Massachusetts (in 1638)] a group in which male citizens of the United States are eligible for membership if presented by a current member or through "Right of Descent" from a previous member.

Ancient and Honorable Order of the Jersey Blues: an organization created in 1960 for male descendants of men who served in the Jersey Blues, resided in New Jersey, or served in the military or judicial service of New Jersey.

ancient demesne: land belonging to the crown in 1066; later, a law passed granting special privileges concerning land.

ancillary: secondary or subordinate to, as in estate administration. *See* ancillary administration.

ancillary administration: secondary administration of an estate which takes place in a state other the one in which the deceased lived.

ancillary letter: letter giving authority for ancillary administration.

ancille: (*obsolete*) a maid servant.

ancome: [*also* whitlow] an ulcerous swelling, a boil.

andesith: (*obsolete*) formerly.

aneurism: a preternatural (abnormal) dilation or rupture of the coats of an artery, either encysted or diffused.

angel: a gold coin ranging in worth from six to ten shillings, given, in the sixteenth century, to those who had partaken in the touching ceremonies for the King's Evil (scrofula).

Angel Bill of Credit: [*also* angel] a bill of public credit issued in 1717 by the Massachusetts Colony, worth ten shillings.

angild: (*obsolete*) a fine or payment to compensate for injury.

angina: general name of the diseases called sore throat, as quinsy, scarlet fever, croup, mumps, etc.

angina pectoris: a dangerous disease, with paroxysms characterized by sudden and severe pain in the lower chest, with a feeling of suffocation.

angle-berry: a fleshy excrescence resembling a large strawberry found on the feet of sheep, cattle, etc.

Anglosajone: Anglo-Saxon— used derogatorily just before the colonization of Spanish Texas.

angwite: [*also* blodwite] a fine paid to settle out of court in cases involving bloodshed.

anile: *literally* "old womanish"; mentally or physically weak; imbecile.

anlepi: alone, single—usually applies to unmarried persons.

annary: an annual record of events.

anni: (*Lat.*) years.

anno: (*Lat.*) in the year.

Anno Domini: (*Lat.*) in the year of our Lord.

annor: (*Lat.*) *see* annus.

anno regni: (*Lat.*) in the year of the reign. *See* regnal years.

annosus: (*Lat.*) aged, old.

annos visit: (*Lat.*) *literally* "he lived [so many] years."

annual rent: another name for the interest on borrowed money.

annuity: a yearly payment.

annulment: in church records, a listing of marriages which were annulled (terminated) shortly after consummation.

Annunciation: [*also* Annuciato Dominica; Lady Day] a feast day of the Roman Catholic Church held on March 25, to commemorate the visit of the Angel Gabriel to the Blessed Virgin Mary, to announce the Incarnation.

annus: (*Lat.*) [*also* annor] year; season; year's produce; age.

annus luctus: (*Lat.*) the year of mourning.

anodyne: drug which will dull pain; analgesic.

anonyma: (*Lat.*) stillborn daughter.

anonymous: lacking a name; of unknown source or origin.

ante: (*Lat.*) before.

ante bellum: usually, the time before the Civil War, 1861-65.

antecessor: (*Lat.*) a predecessor or ancestor.

ante Christian: before Christ

ante diem: (*Lat.*) before the day—used in dating documents.

antehac: (*Lat.*) before this time; earlier.

antenuptial contract or agreement: special arrangements made by couples intending marriage regarding their estates.

anthelmintic: something used to expel or destroy intestinal worms.

anti-abolitionist: one who opposed the abolition of slavery.

antifebrile: a medicine able to abate or cure fever.

Antimission Baptist: one of many Baptist groups named for their opposition to missionary work.

antiparalytic: a medicine used to help palsy victims.

antiperiodic: a medicine which prevented the periodic return of certain diseases, such as malaria.

antipestilential: a substance that will counteract or stop contagion or infection.

antiphlogistic: a remedy used for inflammations.

anti-renter: a person who was opposed to the paying of rent, particularly during the period 1839 to 1850 in New York when the tenants on the estates of the patroon refused to pay feudal fees and render services

antiscorbutic: a remedy used to fight scurvy.

antisialogogue: a medicine used to decrease a heavy flow of saliva—found in medical records.

antispasmodic: a medicine used to reduce muscle cramps or spasms.

antisyphilitic: a medicine used to cure syphilis.

anus: (*Lat.*) old woman.

Apache: Indian tribe of the southwest, particularly New Mexico and Arizona.

a pater: (*Lat.*) from the father.

aperient: laxative.

aphtha: the infantile disease "thrush."

apoline: apoplexy; having to do with a stroke. *See* apoplexy.

apoplexy: hemorrhage of a blood vessel in the brain; a sudden loss of sensation; a stroke.

apostle spoon: old-fashioned silver spoon, the handle of which ends in a figure of the apostles.

Apothecaries' Company: an organization established in England and Wales in 1815 to license apothecary shops. The Worshipful Society of Apothecaries have records dating from 1670 which can be found in the Guildhall Library in London.

apothecary: one who prepared and sold drugs.

Appalachee: a tribe of Indians formerly of northwest Florida.

apparitor: an official of an ecclesiastical court who issues summons and carries out orders of the court.

appeal bond: a bond posted as part of an appeal in review cases.

appearance record: a chronological record, or docket of all cases coming into court.

apprentice: one learning a trade or profession, bound by a contract or other legal agreement to work for a specified length of time under the direction of a master workman in exchange for instruction and learning in the trade, some additional education, and support.

approvement: enclosure of common land by a manor lord.

approver: a person hired to give false witness.

appurtenances: the rights, duties, and perquisites of one who held manorial land—usually, grazing rights, payment of fines, submission to the manorial court, and a pew in church.

a priori: (*Lat.*) from what goes before.

apronman: (*obsolete*) a laboring man; a mechanic.

a quo: (*Lat.*) from where.

Arapaho: central and western plains Indians inhabiting areas around the Platte and Arkansas Rivers.

arbiter: a witness or judge.

archbishop: bishop presiding over a province or diocese.

archdeacon: in the Church of England, a priest who supervises a division or activity of a diocese or archdeaconry.

Arches, Court of: provincial court of appeal of the Archbishop of Canterbury.

archididascalus: (*Lat.*) headmaster.

archipelago: a body of water containing a group of islands.

argentum: (*Lat.*) [*also* argent] silver—often used in heraldic descriptions.

argolet: a mounted bowman.

argosy: a large merchant vessel or fleet of ships.

ariminianism: the Christian theology put forth by Dutch Calvinist Jacobus Arminius (1560-1609), which allows for free will or agency.

Arkansas Indians: an Indian tribe allied with the Dakotas and living along the Ohio River.

armiger: one entitled to bear arms, such as a knight or esquire.

arms: the hereditary armorial bearings of a family with its marks of distinction—as in a coat of arms

army regular: a troop belonging to the army and maintained on a regular basis, as opposed to a volunteer.

arpent: (*obsolete*) "French measure of land, containing a hundred square perches, and varying with the different values of the perch from about an acre and a quarter to about 5/6 of an acre."—*Oxford English Dictionary.*

arpenteur: 1: a land-surveyor. 2: a profession.

arrack: a colonial drink; alcohol or spirits made from rice or molasses.

arraignment: the action of formally bringing charges against someone.

arriere-ban: the act of calling one's vassals to take up arms.

article: a contract, covenant, or other papers of those bound for service and embarking on an overseas journey.

artificer: a blacksmith; one who makes fuses, grenades, shells, etc.

artificial person: a corporation.

ascendant: an ancestor; one who precedes in genealogical succession.

Ascensio: a moveable feast day, Ascension Day is celebrated forty days after Easter.

ascites: a large collection of fluid in the abdominal cavity; dropsy of the abdomen.

asfetidia: [*also* asafetida] a short perennial herb that produces a resinous gum used as an antispasmodic and flavoring.

Ashkenazi: central or eastern European Jews.

askings: the publication of marriage banns, in England, before the twentieth century.

assent to devise: the expressed or implied consent of an executor allowing the title to land to pass to the devisee named in a will.

assessed valuation: official value of property for the purpose of taxation.

assessor: the person whose responsibility it is to decide on the value of property and the rate of tax to be paid, sometimes being the local sheriff or constable.

assign: *see* assignee.

assignation: transferring the administration of an estate from one person to another.

assignee: [*also* assign] a person who has been assigned another's rights or personal property.

assignment: a document transferring land ownership or warrant ownership to another party.

assignment of dower: in probate, a document stipulating the portion of an estate belonging to the widow for her use and the support of her children.

assignment of real estate: *see* decree of distribution.

assignor: an individual who assigns his rights or interests in something to another person.

assistant marshal: [*also* census marshal; census assistant] local census takers prior to 1880 who were assistant to the federal marshals.

assize: 1: in England, an ordinance regulating the weight, measure, and price of articles sold in market. 2: an ancient writ issued from a court of assize for the recovery of property.

associator: in Colonial America, a man willing to go to war. *See* non-associator.

assumpsit: a type of pleading to remedy violations of an agreement.

Assumption: a fixed feast day, celebrating the assumption, or ascent into heaven of the Virgin Mary.

asylum: a place of refuge for the care of orphans and, more usually, for the confinement of the insane.

atavus: (*Lat.*) third great-grandfather; ancestor.

Atherton Gag: from 1838 to 1844, a resolution in Congress stipulating that all bills or petitions dealing with slavery should, without debate, be tabled, which was introduced by C.G. Atherton (1804-53), U.S. Representative and Senator of New Hampshire.

athwart: from side to side; across; against.

atque: (*Lat.*) and, also, even.

atqui: (*Lat.*) but, yet, however, rather.

attachment: a seizure or taking into custody of persons or property, by legal process, to satisfy a court judgment.

attainder: a common law penalty in capital cases by which a convicted felon or traitor lost all civil rights, including the right to hold property.

attest: to bear witness; to affirm as true.

attestation: a certification by oath or signature in the presence of witnesses, corroborating a testimony regarding time of residence, place of residence, employment, family status, ownership of property or goods, etc.

attorney in fact: experienced legal practitioners without technical training who stood as proxy to plead for someone; any mentally competent adult who is authorized to act on the behalf of another.

auditor: court appointed custodian of land and property records.

auger: a tool for boring holes in wood.

aurifex: a goldsmith.

authentic will: *see* notarial will.

automatic citizenship: citizenship granted individuals because of the specific circumstances of the group of which they were a member.

Auxiliary to the Sons of the Union Veterans of the Civil War: a group organized in 1883, originally as the "Ladies Aid Society," for wives and widows of sons of veterans, mothers of sons, and all lineal female descendants.

aver: (*obsolete*) a domestic animal of any kind; a draft ox or horse, especially a horse used for heavy work.

averland: land subject to "average" (one day's work) due to the feudal superior in return for protection.

avia: (*Lat.*) grandmother.

a vinculo: (*Lat.*) *literally* "away from bonds, cords, or chains"; usually regarding divorce.

a vinculo matrimonii: (*Lat.*) *literally* "from the bond of matrimony"; absolute divorce.

avowtrie: (*obsolete*) adultery.

avunculus: (*Lat.*) maternal uncle.

avunculus magnus: (*Lat.*) great-uncle on the mother's side.

avunculus major: (*Lat.*) grandmother's brother, grand-uncle.

avus: (*Lat.*) grandfather; ancestor.

awl: an iron instrument used by shoemakers, saddlers, etc., for piercing, sewing, and stitching.

axes: the ague, generally fits or attacks.

axle-tooth: a molar tooth; a grinder.

Aztec Club of 1847: [*also* The Military Society of the Mexican War (1846-48)] a group organized in 1847 for lineal descendants of commissioned officers of the army, navy, or marine corps serving in Mexico or Mexican waters during the War with Mexico (1846-48).

Azymite: early Christians who first administered the Eucharist with unleavened bread.

B

babery: finery to please a child; any trifling toy for children.

bachelor: an unmarried man; a knight who followed another's standard because he was either too young for his own standard, or he did not have enough followers of his own.

backster: (*obsolete*) originally, a female baker; later, a baker of either sex.

bacteremia: blood poisoning.

badger: [*also, in various dialects* cadger; hawker; huckster] one who buys corn and other commodities and carries them elsewhere to sell; i.e., an itinerant dealer between producer (farmer, fisherman, etc.) and consumer.

baggonet: (*obsolete*) bayonet.

bagman: a travelling salesman; one who shows samples and solicits orders for a manufacturer.

bailiff: in England, an officer under a sheriff who carries out duties involved in arrests and processing criminals.

bailiwick: a district in England under the jurisdiction of a bailiff.

baiting-place: in Colonial America, referring to a stopping-place for rest and food.

bakestre: (*obsolete*) female baker.

balister: (*obsolete*) a cross-bowman.

balm: an aromatic substance consisting of resin mixed with volatile oils, much prized for its fragrance and medicinal properties.

balsam: an aromatic oily medicine used for external application to heal wounds or soothe pain.

ban: formal ecclesiastical denunciation or excommunication.

bandster: (*obsolete*) one who binds sheaves after reapers during a harvest.

bane: that which causes ruin or woe; a curse.

bang beggar: (*slang*) a constable who carries a strong staff.

banker: (*obsolete*) 1: a covering, usually of tapestry, for a bench or chair. 2: a laborer who digs ditches.

bank-rag: paper money.

banks man: 1: an overseer at a coal mine. 2: a bank manager.

bannerere: (*obsolete*) a standard bearer.

bannering: an annual custom of walking the boundaries of a parish to preserve the local jurisdiction and privileges of that particular area.

banns: [*also* intentions] the publication of intended marriages, published for three consecutive Sundays prior to the event.

banqueter: a broker or banker.

bar album: a register of guests at a hotel.

bar mitzvah: Jewish celebration for a boy when he reaches the age of thirteen and is accepted into the congregation.

baratus: (*Lat.*) bearded; adult.

barber-chirurgeon: a person who practiced surgery and was a barber; a low practitioner of surgery.

barbery: (*obsolete*) barber shop.

barkary: (*obsolete*) a sheepcote, a sheep-fold.

barker: (*obsolete*) a tanner.

barkman: a bargeman.

barnage: (*obsolete*) childhood, infancy.

Baron: originally, a feudal tenant granted title to property by a feudal lord or monarch; a British nobleman.

Baroness: the wife of a baron or a lady who holds the title in her own right.

Baronet: a lesser baron; a commoner.

Baron et Feme: husband and wife.

Baronial Order of the Magna Charts: a group organized in **1898** for male descendants **of** the Magna Charta Earls and Barons elected in 1215.

barrator: the master or crew member of a ship who commits barratry. *See* barratry.

28

barratry: the encouraging of lawsuits and quarrels in an attempt to cheat or defraud ship owners or insurers, such as sinking, deserting, or embezzling the cargo of a ship.

barrel fever: sickness produced by immoderate drinking.

barrel weight: a measure of weight being equal to 196 pounds.

barrister: an English lawyer or one who works in the courts.

barrow: 1: a mound of earth or stones erected over a grave. 2: a castrated boar. 3: a long, sleeveless garment for a baby made of flannel.

berth: (*obsolete*) a warm sheltered place for cattle or sheep.

baseborn: referring to a child born to parents of humble means; referring to one born of an illegitimate union.

baseline: the first or beginning east-west running line laid out in each of thirty-seven different surveys in the public domain states.

base-son: an illegitimate child.

base tenant: one who performed lowly or inferior services for his landlord.

bason: in hat making, a workbench with a slab of iron or stone flag on it and a small fire underneath, used for the first part of the felting process.

bastardy bond: a bond posted by the father of an illegitimate child to ensure that the child is supported without public expense.

bastille: a castle tower or small fortress; a wooden tower on wheels for the protection of the troops; a notorious prison built in Paris which was destroyed in 1789.

bateau: a light, flat-bottomed boat used on rivers and propelled by long oars or poles.

bat mitzvah: Jewish celebration for a girl when she reaches the age of thirteen and is accepted into the congregation.

bawd: a procurer or procuress for a house of prostitution; one who conducted criminal intrigues and provided women for lewd purposes.

bawdy-house: a brothel.

baxter: (*obsolete*) a baker.

bayman: 1: resident of the Massachusetts Bay Colony. 2: a Yankee fishing ship.

bayou: a stream forming a sluggish and marshy outlet or inlet to a larger body of water.

beaconage: money paid to maintain a beacon.

beadle: a town crier or warrant officer; a lowly parish officer appointed to keep order in church, punish petty offenders, and act as a servant or messenger of the parish.

beakiron: the tapered end of a blacksmith's anvil.

beal: a pimple; a pustule.

beaming knife: a tanner's tool used in beaming or taking the hair off a hide.

beamster: the man who works at the beam in a tannery. *See* beaming knife.

bearer: in heraldry, a figure in an achievement placed by the side of a shield in supportive position, usually the figure of a beast.

bearing cloth: a child's christening robe or blanket.

bearing tree: in surveying, a tree marked or blazed to indicate boundaries.

bea: (*obsolete*) domesticated farm animal.

beat: county subdivision in Mississippi and other states.

bechic: pectoral; a medicine for relieving coughs.

bed and board, from: legal separation of man and wife, without final divorce—separation from bed and board.

bedder: 1: an upholsterer. 2: one who takes care of the breeding or birthing of cattle. 3: a bedmaker.

bedehouse: a hospital; an alms house.

bed-swerver: (*Victorian*) a person who is unfaithful to the marriage vow.

Beecher's Bible: a Sharp's rifle named after Reverend Henry Ward Beecher who raised funds to purchase Sharp's rifles for anti-slavery emigrants settling the west in the 1800s.

beefeater: (*British*) a yeoman of the guard; a well-fed servant.

bee gum: a hollowed gum tree used as a beehive.

beest: (*obsolete*) beast.

beetle: a toot consisting of a heavy weight or head, usually of wood, for driving wedges, and ramming down paving stones, etc.

beldam: [*also* beldame] a great-grandmother; a woman who has lived to see five generations of female descendants; a hideous old hag.

belfry: 1: a bell tower. 2: a shelter for cattle.

belladonna: a medicine to calm the digestive system, derived from the Deadly Nightshade plant.

bellman: a town crier employed to make public announcements in the streets.

bellwether: the sheep at the head of a flock.

belshire: a grandfather; an ancestor.

bench mark: a surveyor's mark cut in durable material to indicate levels for determining altitudes.

bench warrant: a court order issued for an arrest upon the failure of a witness to appear in court.

benefice: 1: a church office, such as a rector, and the income provided by such an office. 2: land held by a feudal tenant because of services rendered.

beneficial ownership/use: the use of property by a beneficiary even though he or she is not the legal owner of the property—found in probate records.

benefit of clergy: exemption from secular court given to the clergy in certain criminal cases.

bene quiescat: (*Lat.*) may he rest well.

bene visit: (*Lat.*) he lived a good life.

bequeath: to give personal property by means of a will; to hand down.

bequest: a gift, personal property, or money handed down in a will.

berg: a borough or town.

berner: (*obsolete*) a man in charge of a pack of hounds.

besom maker: (*obsolete*) 1: one who makes brooms. 2: contemptuously, a low woman.

bespoke work: custom made articles.

Bethlehem: a hospital for the mentally ill.

bethlehemite: 1: a mentally ill person. 2: in 1257 the Bethlehemites were a quasi-monastic order.

better: a person who was higher on a social scale than another.

bettering house: a reformatory or charitable organization essentially for the sick and poor; a workhouse for keeping wayward persons.

bevel: a common joiner's and mason's tool which had a fiat rule with a moveable tongue or arm jointed at one end for measuring and marking angles.

bibliopolist: one who deals in rare books.

bibliothecary: a librarian.

bibliotheke: a library or book collection.

bid-stand: (*obsolete*) one who bids travelers to "stand and deliver"; a highwayman or robber.

biennium: a period of two years.

bier: the moveable stand on which a corpse is placed before burial.

bier-balk: church road for burials.

bierne: (*obsolete*) warrior.

bilander: a small merchant vessel with two masts, distinguished from other vessels of two masts by the form of the main-sail.

bilbo: a long iron bar used as a hobble for prisoners.

bilious: having an undue amount of bile.

bilious fever: a fever supposed to be due to a liver disorder.

bill: an instrument used by plumbers, basket makers, and gardeners used for pruning trees, hedges, etc.; (*obsolete*) a pick-axe or battle-axe.

bill hook: a heavy knife with a hooked end used for pruning, cutting brush wood, etc.

binding day: the second Tuesday after Easter.

binding out: the act of apprenticing or indenturing children.

biretta: the square cap worn by clerics of the Roman Catholic Church.

bis: (*Lat.*) twice; a duplicate.

bisextile: pertaining to leap year; every fourth year.

bistoury: surgical instrument for making incisions.

bitters: a tonic made of alcohol and a vegetable infusion.

black-coat: clergyman; parson.

Black Cross Day: St. Mark's Day, April 25th.

Black Death: *see* black plague.

black drink: a drink made of leaves used by the Indians of the southern United States as a ceremonial drink and as a medicine.

Black Law: a law regulating the admission of blacks into a state or territory.

black plague: [*also* Black Death] a form of bubonic plague.

black pox: black smallpox.

black-pudding: a food made of blood and grain.

black rent: rents paid in corn

black-pudding: a food made of blood and grain.

black rent: rents paid in corn and meat instead of money.

Black Sunday: Passion Sunday.

black fin: 1: tin ore that is dressed, stamped, and washed ready for melting. 2: black powder.

black vomit: vomiting caused by the presence of old blood in the stomach due to conditions such as a bleeding ulcer or yellow fever.

blanch farm: rent paid to the lord of a manor in silver, rather than service, labor, or produce.

blanch-holding: a tenure whereby the tenant pays only a small yearly duty to his superior as an acknowledgment to his right.

blemmere: (*pre-nineteenth* century) a plumber.

bletonist: one who possesses the ability to perceive water underground by sensation.

blinky milk: sour milk.

blocker: 1: a tool for blocking. 2: a small piece of meat for sale on the butcher's block.

blodwile: *see* angwite.

bloman: a negro or blackamoor (an African negro).

blood stone: a stone worn as an amulet and thought to be a preventive for nosebleeds.

bloody flux: dysentery; discharges from the bowels mixed with blood.

bloody sweat: 1: a sweat accompanied by a discharge of blood. 2: a disease called sweating sickness.

bloomery: the first forge in an iron-works through which the melted metal passes.

bloughty: swollen

blown: swollen or inflated.

blown meat: maggot infested meat.

blue coat: 1: the dress of servants and the lower orders. 2: almoners and children on charity.

blue law: a very strict colonial law which prohibited such activities as dancing, shows, and sports on Sunday.

blue light: a New England federalist against the War of 1812.

bluffer: a landlord.

boaster: a broad-faced chisel used by masons to smooth the surface of a stone.

boatswain: an officer in charge of the sails and rigging.

bobbin: 1: a spool of thread or yarn. 2: a small bundle or fagot of firewood.

bocher: (*obsolete*) butcher.

bodily heir: a natural-born child, grandchild, or other descendant.

bodkin: 1: a dagger; 2: a type of rich cloth; 3: awl-like toot used to pick out letters in correcting set-up type.

bole: 1: a small square recess in the wall of a room used as a small shelf; a small opening in the wall of a castle or cottage to let in light and air. 2: a smelter for refining lead.

boll: a measure for grain.

boiler: a drunkard.

bolus: a larger than ordinary pill.

bon: good; sufficient in law.

bona: (*Lat.*) movable property.

bona fide: (*Lat.*) in good faith.

bona notabilia: (*Lat.*) considerable goods.

bonded passenger: passengers convicted of various crimes.

bondmaid: a female slave; a bound servant not due wages.

bondman: a male slave; one bound to service without wages.

bond servant: *see* indentured servant.

bondsman: a person who will vouch for or be liable for a sum of money if a person fails to appear in court.

boneset: a willow-like plant, the leaves of which were used as a medicine or tea.

bone-shave: [*also* boneshaw] sciatica, hip-gout.

bonny-clabber: milk that has become thick in the process of souring.

bookholder: a theatrical prompter.

bookman: student.

Boones's Trace: [*also* Wilderness Road] an early road or trace in Kentucky from the Cumberland Gap to Boonesborough.

boot-catcher: the person at an inn whose business was to pull off boots.

born in the covenant: in LDS records, one born to a couple who has been sealed in marriage, and thus is sealed to the parents.

borstax: (*obsolete*) an axe.

botcher: a cobbler; a tailor; an unskillful laborer.

boteler: (*obsolete*) butler.

bottoming tool: a narrow, rather concave shovel used by drainers.

bottomry: [*also* hypothecation] the mortgaging of a ship to obtain a loan, whereby the ship then becomes collateral or security for the loan.

bottony: in heraldry, a cross which terminates at each end in three buds, knots, or buttons.

boulting mill: a mill for refining flour further by sifting the bran out; part of a grist mill.

boumet: (*obsolete*) to embalm.

bound: being obligated to serve another for payment, passage, instruction in a trade, etc., in return.

boundary rider: one who rode boundary fences on property to make sure they were in good repair.

bounde: (*obsolete*) a husbandman (farmer) or peasant.

bounder: 1: one who marks or sets boundaries. 2: a socially unacceptable person.

bound out: the condition of apprenticed or indentured children.

bounds: natural, man-made, or artificial physical features such as water courses, shore lines, fences, roads, trees, rock that define the boundaries of a parcel of land.

bounty: a gift or compensation offered for some specified action or service (e.g., bounty money or land); a reward bestowed on an individual soldier for an act of heroism.

bounty land: land designated as payment for military service.

bounty land warrant: a right to free land in the public domain; the certificate, to satisfy the law, showing time served, unit (regiment or corps), and where served.

bout: the distance from one side of a field to the other, and back again, when ploughing.

bovate: a land measure known as an oxgang, or as much land as one ox could plough in a year, varying in amount from ten to eighteen acres.

bowcer: *see* bowser.

bowchyer: (*obsolete*) butcher.

bowel complaint: any gastro-intestinal disorder.

bower maiden: *see* burmaiden.

bowery: a farm or plantation.

bowie knife: a steel hunting knife with a single edge about fifteen inches long, invented by Colonel James Bowie.

bowyer: (*archaic*) a person in the bow trade; an archer.

Boxing Day: the first week-day after Christmas Day.

brachygrapher: a person who writes short hand.

Braddock's Road: an early route to the West from Baltimore, Maryland to Wheeling, West Virginia. *See* Nemcolin's Path.

brad: 1: a small nail. 2: (*slang*) money.

braidery: embroidery.

brake: 1: an instrument of torture. 2: a baker's trough for kneading dough.

brash: fragile, brittle wood, too brittle to be used in basket weaving.

brasier: [*also* brazier] a brass worker.

breakbone: dengue fever.

brennage: a tribute paid to the lord by his tenants instead of the obligatory bran for his hounds.

Brethren church: [*also* Dunkers; Tunkers; Dunkards; River Brethren; Brethren in Christ; The Brethren Church (Progressive Brethren and Grace Brethren); Church of United Brethren in Christ] generally, the group of German pietists who believed in the Anabaptist teachings of baptism by immersion of responsible individuals, not infants.

Bretheren of Christ: *see* Christidelphians.

brevet: honorary military rank.

brewster: a female brewer.

Brewsterite: *see* Cutlerite.

brick keel: (*archaic*) a brick kiln.

bridges: (*obsolete*) brudges (satin).

brigant: (*obsolete*) brigand; a bandit or robber.

Brighamite: a nickname given to a follower of Brigham Young.

Bright's disease: inflammation of the kidney.

Brinser: a follower of Matthias Brinser who, in 1855, led in organizing United Zion's Children.

bris: Jewish circumcision.

broadcloth: plain-woven, double-width black cloth used mostly for men's clothing.

broadhorn boat: a flat river boat for carrying coal.

broadside: a newspaper or poster placed in a public place, for announcements.

brocour: (*obsolete*) a broker.

bromide paper: the predecessor of present day photographic paper introduced in the 1890s in a variety of textures using blue or blue-black tones and having a bronzed metallic silver look.

bronchocele: enlarged thyroid gland.

bronze John: yellow fever.

broom squire: persons involved in the manufacture of brooms.

Brumaire: month of fog.

brunswick dress: a riding-dress for ladies, with a jacket resembling a man's in construction.

bucket shop: 1: a place where liquor could be purchased and put in buckets, bottles, etc., brought by the patrons. 2: a brokerage firm that holds the money of the customer rather than purchasing his order.

buck washer: a laundress.

buffalo soldier: a black soldier serving in the American west.

buffalo trace: a road or path made by buffalo herds used as roads by frontiersmen and pioneers.

buffer: a persons who took a false oath for a consideration.

bule: (*obsolete*) boil, tumor, or swelling.

bullwhacker: a bullock-driver; one who drove bullocks (oxen).

bummer: a soldier who deserted the ranks to raid and plunder without discrimination.

bundling: a custom involving persons of the opposite sex sleeping in the same bed with their clothes on.

bunker: the coal bin of a steam-driven vessel.

bunter: a rag and bone woman.

burger register: a Swiss or German register which lists persons having citizenship in a given town known as a "Burg," hence a resident is a "burger."

burgess: a delegate, freeman, or representative in a borough.

burgundy pitch: a yellow brown, hard, sticky resin prepared from the sap of Norway Spruce trees used in medicinal plasters.

burler: one who dresses or readies cloth for sale by removing flaws, knots, or imperfections.

burmaiden: [*also* bower-maiden] a chambermaid or lady in waiting.

burness: a man of New Sweden (a section along the Delaware River) who cleared land by burning, directly disobeying a Swedish law which did not allow land to be cleared by burning.

burse: (*obsolete*) a place where merchants met for transacting business.

busheler: a tailor's assistant.

busker: (*obsolete*) a hairdresser.

bustum: (*Lat.*) tomb, sepulchre.

buttery book: a book containing the names of members of a college and the account of their commons.

butterice: a farrier's tool used to shape or pare a horse's hoof.

C

cabinet print: a large size (4 x 7 inches) albumen photograph on card stock.

cabin-parloured: a home with a parlour not larger than a cabin on a ship.

Cable Act: in 1922, a revision to naturalization laws in which not wives were not allowed to become citizens upon marriage, the residency requirement was reduced to one year, and the Declaration of Intention could be waived.

cable length: a unit of measurement, approximately 100 fathoms; marine charts measure the length at 607 degrees, fifty-six feet, or one-tenth of a sea mile.

cabossed: in heraldry, the head of any beast facing front with no neck showing, exceptions being a lion, which is called a "face" and a fox, which is called a "mask."

cabriolet: a two-wheeled chaise pulled by one horse, having a top of wood or leather, and a large apron to cover the lap and legs.

caccagague: an ointment made of alum and honey, used as a laxative.

cachere: (*obsolete*) a hunter.

cachet: a seal.

cachexy: an extreme condition of the body caused by malnutrition.

cacogastric: an upset stomach.

cacopathy: (*obsolete*) a severe affliction or malady.

cacospysy: (*obsolete*) a bad or irregular pulse rhythm.

cacotrophy: condition of the body due to poor nutrition.

cadastre: a register kept for taxation purposes containing amount, value, and ownership of land; a poll (head) tax record of those qualifying to vote; a Domesday book.

cadaver: (*Lat.*) corpse.

caddie: a man in pursuit of an odd job as messenger, errand-boy, errand porter, etc.; more specifically, a member of a corps of commissionaires in eighteenth-century Edinburgh.

caddis: [*also* caddis ribbon] cotton, wool, or floss silk used in padding; lint used in surgery; a worsted tape or binding used for garters.

cadette: a younger daughter or sister.

cadger: originally, a person who carried caged hawks, falcons, or other birds for sale; a packman or itinerant huckster; one who travels from town to town selling farm produce and dairy products, collected from farms, to sell to town dwellers. *See* badger.

cado: (*Lat.*) to be slain; to abate, decay, end, or fail.

cadre: permanent group of men who form the basic framework of a regiment.

caducous: subject to falling sickness or epilepsy.

caedes: (*Lat.*) slaughter; murder.

caelebs: (*Lat.*) [*also* coelebs] unmarried (bachelor or widower).

caffa: a silk cloth similar to damask.

cag: (*obsolete*) keg; a small barrel.

Cahokia: a French fort established in 1699 in the Mississippi Valley.

cairn: a pyramid made of stones used as a boundary marker or burial monument.

Cajun: (*corruption of the word Acadian*) persons of French descent living in Louisiana.

cakewalk: a parade or walkaround where one's fanciest dance steps were displayed and the winner received a cake.

calash: a light carriage with low wheels and a removable folding top; a woman's hood made of silk with whalebone or cane hoops.

calcar: 1: (*obsolete*) a diviner. 2: a small furnace used in glassmaking.

calcimining brush: a brush used to apply whitewash.

calefacient: a medical agent that produces warmth or a sense of heat.

calefactory: a warming pan; a ball of precious metal containing hot water; a room in a monastery in which to get warm.

calends: the first day of any month in the Roman calendar.

calibogus: a drink consisting of a mixture of rum and spruce beer.

caligo: 1: dimming of the sight. 2: dark or obscure.

caliphe: a sailing vessel.

calker: an astrologer or magician.

calligraphy: beautiful, elegant penmanship practiced as an art or profession.

callimanco: a fashionable woolen material.

calliope: a musical instrument similar to an organ but using a series of steam whistles to make music.

calliper: a compass for measuring the diameter of convex bodies and the bore or internal diameter of tubes.

calmative: sedative.

calo: (*Lat.*) a soldier's servant.

calomel: a purgative or laxative made from mercurous chloride.

calotype: [*also* Talbotype] a process developed in 1839 by Fox Talbot, that used negatives to make positive prints on paper.

Cambellites: a religious group named for its founders, Thomas and Alexander Campbell.

cambist: a banker or one who deals in notes and bills.

cambric: fine white linen used in making handkerchiefs.

camerist: a lady's maid.

camlet: a soft material (silk or wool) used especially for cloaks and petticoats.

campane: in heraldry, furnished or adorned with bells.

campestres: (*obsolete*) for pastures or open fields.

camp fever: typhus.

camphor: an odorous substance used in pharmacy products, formerly as an anti-aphrodisiac.

camphor cerate: a preparation for external application consisting of wax, camphor, and other medicinal ingredients used in treating colds.

can: [*also* cann] a tankard or mug, with or without a lid.

Candlemas: the feast of purification of the Virgin Mary and Presentation of the Lord celebrated on February 2.

candle-rent: (*obsolete*) rent or revenue obtained from house property.

candle-shears: snuffer.

candlewood set: a splinter of resinous wood burned to give light.

candy man: 1: an itinerant candy salesman. 2: (*England*) a bailiff or process server.

canine madness: hydrophobia (rabies).

cankery: gangrenous

cannaller: a person who worked or lived on a canal boat.

canon: an ecclesiastical ruling or law.

canon law: ecclesiastical law.

canons of descent: laws governing inheritance.

cant: language used by gypsies, thieves, professional beggars, etc., for secrecy; an auction chant or singing musical sound.

Cantate: a moveable feast day, the forth Sunday after Easter.

cant-dog: *see* cant-hook.

canter: 1: a speaker using professional or religious cant. 2: also a nickname for the Puritans in the seventeenth century.

cant-hook: [*also* cant-dog] a lever used for canting or turning timber that consisted of a wooden bar with an iron catch or hooked arm near the bottom.

canting caller: an auctioneer.

canton: in heraldry, an ordinary of a shield or escutcheon, being a square division less then a quarter, occupying the upper (usually dexter) corner of the shield.

Canuck: a French Canadian.

canus: (*Lat.*) gray; old age.

cape merchant: the head merchant in a factory.

caper: a cap maker.

capias: (*Lat.*) *see* writ of capias.

capitation tax: head or poll tax, based upon population.

captain's district: [*also* captain's "company"] subdivision of a county.

caput: (*Lat.*) head or top; source, such as of rivers.

Caput Jejunii, dies cinerum: a moveable feast day, Ash Wednesday, the first day of Lent.

carder: one who cards wool.

carding: the dressing or combing of wool, cotton, etc., by hand or in a carding machine.

Caresme: Lent.

carl: a country man; one of low birth or rude manners.

carnifex: (*obsolete*) an executioner or butcher.

caroche: a luxurious coach or chariot.

carpetbagger: northerner who went south after the Civil War and tried, by the black vote or otherwise, to obtain political influence—generally applied to anyone interfering with the policies of a locality where he has no permanent or genuine connection.

carriage: a tax or toll on the transport of goods through a country or territory.

carte-de-visit: an albumen type photograph mounted on card stock.

carter: a wagoner, stable headman, or charioteer.

cartwright: one who made carts or wagons.

caruage: ploughing.

carucate: a measure of land, it was as much as could be tilled with a team of eight oxen in one year.

cash land: public land sold for cash.

cashmarie: one who transports fish from the coast to markets inland. *See* rippier.

castellet: a small castle.

catabaptist: one who rejected the orthodox doctrine of baptism. *See* Anabaptist.

catal: (*obsolete*) cattle.

catalepsy: a disease characterized by a seizure or trance wherein sensation and consciousness are suspended.

catarrh: cerebral hemorrhage or apoplexy, it later came to mean an inflammation of the mucous membrane which caused profuse running of the eyes and nose.

catarrh epidemic: influenza.

catchpole: [*also* catchpolla] sheriff's assistant or warrant officer who arrests debtors; a bailiff.

catechumen: a new convert receiving instruction in a religion before baptism.

cater-cousin: persons who were cousinly, intimate friends, or very familiar with each other, but who were not cousins by blood.

catgut: a cloth used for lining garments and embroidery.

cathartic: a purgative or strong laxative.

catshead hammer: a hammer with a broad head.

causa mortis: (*Lat.*) in anticipation or contemplation of approaching death.

causary: dismissal from military service due to ill health.

causey: 1: an embankment to retain a river or pond. 2: a raised footpath beside a carriage road likely to be submerged in extreme weather.

causidic: (*obsolete*) lawyer or attorney.

cautioner: one who gives or becomes security for another person.

cavalier: a person who fought on the side of Charles I in his war against Parliament in the seventeenth century.

caveat: a formal notice to a court or magistrate to suspend or prevent probate before the dissenting party could be heard.

cedula: a decree or order.

cense: a tax or tribute.

censeo: (*Lat.*) to count, reckon, or tax.

census marshall: [*also* census assistant] *see* assistant marshall.

cephalic: a medicine for headache or other disorders of the head; pertaining to the head.

cere cloth: a cloth smeared or saturated with wax or glutinous matter and used for wrapping a dead body.

cert-money: an annual fine paid by the tenants of a manor for the certain keeping of the Leet (court).

cession: yielding or surrendering rights or property.

cestue que use: (*French*) a person whose property was transferred for the benefit of another.

cestui que trust: (*French*) a person with a right to a trust or the beneficiary of a trust.

cestui que vie: (*French*) a life estate transferred to a person.

chain: a lineal measure of land of 66 feet, 100 links of chain, or 4 poles, and equal to 1/80 of a mile.

chain of title: the successive conveyances of title (ownership) to a certain property, starting with the patent or other original source and ending with the present holder or title bearer.

chair bodger: an itinerant craftsman who mended or made new parts for chairs.

chaise: a four-wheeled, horse drawn, enclosed carriage for transporting mail, passengers, and a few goods.

chalk: (late *seventeenth century*) 25 cents—$1.25 was five chalks, for example.

chalk-stone: a calcarious (chalky) deposit in the hands and feet of men affected by the gout.

chamber and key: *see* cove and key.

chamberer: a chamber maid or one who frequents ladies' chambers (a gallant).

chambermaid: a female servant who attends to the bedrooms in a house or inn.

chambermaster: a shoemaker who works in his own home.

chamoising: the practice of preparing leather to resemble chamois skin.

chandler: originally, one who made or sold candles; a retail dealer in provisions, groceries, etc.

chandry: a place in the home where candles were kept.

change house: a small inn or alehouse

chantry: small chapel attached to a parish church.

chapman: an itinerant peddler or one who keeps a booth in a marketplace.

charet: a carriage or cart.

chareter: the driver of a charet; a horse that draws a charet.

charge-house: a boarding school.

charnel house: a vault or house under or near a church where bones of the dead are kept.

charter chest: a small chest used to keep important papers.

charterer: a freeholder; one who holds land by charter.

charter party: an indenture or written contract on a single sheet that is torn or cut in two pieces with each man having a part so it could be fitted and matched later.

chartulary: an officer who had the care of charters and other papers of a public nature.

charwoman: a cleaning woman hired by the day.

chatelaine: 1: (*medieval*) the mistress of a castle or country house. 2: later, the ornament women wore to represent the keys of a medieval chatelaine.

chattel: any kind of moveable personal property.

chemise: [*also* shift] a woman's shirt-like undergarment.

chester: 1: a city or walled town. 2: one who puts a corpse into a coffin.

chevalier: in heraldry, a horse-man armed at all points.

chief: 1: in heraldry, the head or upper part of the escutcheon representing a man's head. 2: tenure in chief refers to land held by a tenant that belonged to the king.

chief rent: a rent paid under a tenure in chief, later called quit rent.

chilblain: an inflammatory swelling of the hands and feet caused by exposure to cold.

childbed fever: an infection following the birth of a child; puerperal fever.

Children's Aid Societies: programs established by government, church, or private agencies to benefit poor children.

chillumchee: a wash basin made of brass or tinned copper.

chiminage: a toll paid for the right of passage through a forest.

chimney-money: hearthmoney; a duty or tax (two shillings per annum) paid for each chimney or hearth.

chimney sweep: a small boy or other person hired to clean out chimneys.

chin-cough: a contagious disease, sometimes called whooping cough, characterized by breathing difficulties, and in its worst stage, convulsions.

Chinese Exclusion Act: 1882 act passed to withhold citizenship from the many Chinese immigrants who had come to work on the railroad.

Chinook: an Indian tribe which lived on the Columbia river; the jargon which resulted from the attempts of the employees of the Hudson Bay company to relate to the Indians in the area.

chiragrical: being subject to gout or having gout in the hand.

chirograph: [*also* chirography] an indenture or charter party; a deed of conveyance or a bond given in one's own handwriting.

chiropodist: 1: one required to buy a permit or license thus contributing through indirect tax. 2: one who treats diseases of the hands and feet.

chirurgeon: [*also* chirugeon] a surgeon.

chit: a signed note, usually for food or lodging.

chiv: a knife.

chlorosis: the sickness common to females and characterized by a pale or greenish hue of the skin, weakness, palpitation, and dyspepsia.

choak-damp: [*also* choke-damp] carbonic acid gas that accumulates in old coal-pits, the bottom of wells, quarries, and caves.

cholagogue: a medicine for diminishing excess bile.

cholecystitis: inflammation of the gall bladder.

cholelithiasis: stones in the gallbladder or bile duct.

chop-church: [*also* church-chopper] a secular priest who would trade or take advantage by exchanging benefices.

chopper: one who barters or exchanges, especially ecclesiastical benefices.

chorea: St. Vitus's dance, the dancing madness (choreomania); an epidemic characterized by contortions, convulsions, and dancing.

chowder: (*obsolete*) jowder or jowter, a fish seller.

Christadelphians: [*also* Brethren or Brothers of Christ; Thomasites] a group founded in

1848 by John Thomas, a member of the Disciples of Christ.

Christian and Missionary Alliance: a group founded by a Presbyterian pastor A.B. Simpson in 1881 in New York, known as the Gospel Tabernacle Church.

Christ-tide: Christmas.

cloister: (*Lat.*) a monastery, convent; the covered walk surrounding a church or cathedral.

cloom: sticky mud or clay.

close: enclosed land around or beside a building, courtyard, farm yard, or the precinct of a cathedral.

Close Rolls: letters, private deeds, or conveyances, copied and stitched together in long rolls and sealed.

closet and key: *see* cove and key.

clyster: a medicine injected into the rectum which cleansed the bowels and afforded nutrition; an enema.

coal-heaver: one who unloaded coal from ships.

coaly: a coal-heaver.

coasting-trade: trade carried on between different ports of the same country or jurisdiction.

coatee: a tight-fitting coat or jacket with short tails used mostly in the military.

cobbler: 1: a drink made of wine, sugar, fruit juice, and crushed ice. 2: a shoemaker.

cochen: (*obsolete*) cushion.

Cochranite: member of a religious movement begun in Maine by Jacob Cochran in 1816.

cocket: a royal seal or a scroll of parchment sealed and delivered by the officers of the customhouse to merchants as verification that their merchandise had cleared.

cockney: 1: the dialect of London. 2: a prudish woman.

cock's comb: cap worn by a professional fool resembling a cock's comb in shape and color.

cod: a pillow or cushion.

codicil: a supplement or an addition to a will.

codman: 1: a fish seller. 2: the name for a vessel used in cod-fishery.

coelebs: *see* caelebs.

Coetus: an organization to bring together scattered German and Dutch Reform Churches in America, created by Swiss minister, Michael Schlatter in 1747.

cofferer: a treasurer; an officer in the royal household in England, just beneath the controller in authority.

coffle: a group of slaves chained together.

cogmen: men who bought and sold a coarse cloth called cogware.

cogname: *see* cognomen.

cognate: (*Scottish*) a relation on the mother's side.

cognati: (*Lat.*) related by birth; related on the mother's side.

cognomen: [*a/so* cogname] surname or family name.

cohabitation: the act of living together publicly as husband and wife.

coillor: (*obsolete*) a collector.

coistsell: a groom in charge of the care of a knight's horses.

cold plague: a kind of ague in which the body suffered extreme chills.

collarage: a tax assessed for the collars of wine-drawing horses.

collateral consanguinity: persons who have the same ancestors but do not descend from one another, such as uncle and nephew.

college scrip: land scrip issued and sold to establish colleges.

collier: a coal miner or coal merchant; a vessel used for the transportation of coal.

colona: (*Lat.*) country woman.

Colonial Dames of America: founded in 1890 for women descended from an ancestor who served one of the thirteen original colonies in a public office or in the armed forces.

Colonial Order of the Acorn: a group organized in 1894 for males of lineal descent of residents of an American Colony prior to 4 July 1776.

Colonial Society of Pennsylvania: a society incorporated in 1895 for males over the age of twenty-one lineally descended from a colonist who settled in America before 1900.

colonus: (*Lat.*) husbandman, farmer.

colporteur: an itinerant book salesman, most often one employed by a society to travel about and sell or distribute Bibles and religious writings.

comber: a person who combed wool; a machine for combing the fibers of cotton or wool to make very fine yam.

comfit: sweetened dried fruit.

common: an open ground which is used by all the inhabitants of a community.

common law marriage: a marriage without ceremony, civil or ecclesiastical, which may or may not be recognized as a legal marriage.

common law wife: a woman living with a man, in all appearances his wife, but without having had a legal ceremony.

common plea: civil action at law brought by one subject against another.

commother: the relationship of a godmother to the other godparents and the parents of a child.

compier: (*obsolete*) compeer, an associate or companion of equal rank or standing.

compline: one of the seven canonical hours, it is the last service of the day.

compos mentis: (*Lat.*) of sound mind.

comprizing bill: a summation of charges.

comprobate: to prove or sanction.

compt: (*Lat.*) county.

concern: estate; a business organization.

Concord coach: a vehicle, commonly known as a stagecoach, manufactured in Concord, New Hampshire around 1820.

concords: an agreement, made by permission of the court, between the parties when a fine is in consideration.

condemned land: private property taken for public use and compensated justly under laws governing eminent domain.

conditional will: a will which depends on some uncertain event taking place—marriage between two specific persons for example.

conditio: (*Lat.*) condition; situation; agreement; marriage; married person.

confectionery: a maker of sweets; sometimes, one who makes medicines or poisons.

confession: 1: a statement of the religious beliefs of a religious body. 2: an admission of sin.

confined: 1: constipated. 2: a laborer, hired by the year.

confinement: child-birth; the period before the birth of a child when a woman was confined to her house.

confiner: one who lives near the border of a county.

confirmand: in church records, a person who is to be confirmed.

confirmation: 1: the completion of the probate by the executors. 2: a ceremony by which a new person is accepted into a church.

congeable: (*obsolete*) lawful, lawfully done, or allowable.

congestion: the accumulation of matter in the body such as in abscesses or tumors; the accumulation of blood in one part of the body.

congestive chills/fever: malaria.

congius: ancient Roman measure for liquids, about six pints.

Congress lands: lands sold by officers of the government by enactment of the laws of Congress.

conjoined: united.

conjoint will: *see* joint will.

conjugal: pertaining to marriage or the married state.

conjugium: (*Lat.*) 1: marriage; wedlock. 2: husband.

conjunx: (*Lat.*) wife.

conjux: (*Lat.*) spouse; wife; bride; husband.

Connecticut Western Reserve: 3,840,000 acres in northeastern Ohio between Lake Erie and Pennsylvania.

connor: one who tests, examines, or inspects.

conquest: an inheritance acquired by purchase or gift and not by true inheritance.

consanguineous: (*Lat.*) related by blood; brotherly, sisterly.

consanguinity: the relationship or connection of persons descended from a common ancestor; blood relationship.

consensual marriage: common-law marriage.

consensus, non concubitus facit nuptias: (*Lat.*) consent, not cohabitation, makes marriage.

conservator: a person appointed by the court to take care of the income from the estate of a person who is judged incompetent or who is a minor, which income is used for the support of the incompetent or minor.

conservator pacis: keeper of the peace.

consistory: a church or civil council or court.

consistoryman: an official in a church, possibly a record keeper.

consobrina: (*Lat.*) first cousin on the father's side.

consobrinus: (*Lat.*) cousin.

consort: companion; a wife or husband; spouse; mate.

constat de persona: (*Lat.*) *literally* "here is proof of the person."

construction: to interpret or make clear a legal document.

constructive grant: a land grant of the English Crown not under English law, because the title was subject to the right of occupancy.

constructive notice: the notice with which a person is charged because of documents filed in public records.

consul: one appointed by his government to live in another country, represent his govern-ment, and provide services for citizens of his country who also live there.

consular court: the court of merchants and sea-going trad-ers established in cities with heavy maritime business; the court held for the settlement of civil cases by consuls.

consummate: to finish or achieve that which is begun—a wife's dower right becomes con-summate upon her husband's death; a husband's curtesy right becomes consummate on the death of his wife.

consumption: pulmonary tu-berculosis; a wasting away of the body, particularly by the dis-ease called phthisis pulmonalia.

contagion: *see* corruption.

contemporaneous: existing, living, or occurring at the same time as another event or an-other person.

contested will: a will which one of the heirs finds reason to be-lieve is not correct and thus con-tests it—if the mental condition of the maker can be brought into question or some form of fraud can be established the will is declared contested.

continental: one who supported the revolution in the America; of or belonging to the colonists; during and immediately after the War of Independence.

continental establishment: those who served the cause of the union during the Revolutionary War in any of its organizations.

continental line: the regular Army of the United States during the American Revolution.

contingent: in land records, rights to accrue on the happening of a future event.

contingent estate: an estate which is passed down to heirs based on an event happening.

continuation: gaiters (cloth or leather coverings for the instep and ankle, which sometimes continued up the leg over the calf) continuous with knee breeches.

contraband: 1: goods prohibited by law or treaty from being imported or exported; 2: a Negro that escaped from slavery.

contraband camp: a place where slaves were kept during and after the Civil War to await assistance in getting started by the Freedman's Bureau.

conubium: (*Lat.*) marriage.

convertible: something that can be exchanged for a specified equivalent, as a bond or money.

convey: the transfer of title of property to another, by a written document such as a deed; to transfer ownership.

conveyance: the legal document by which the title of property or land is transferred.

convinced Friend: one admitted to membership in the Society of Friends (Quakers) at their own request.

convocation: a Protestant Episcopal ecclesiastical jurisdiction or district, usually made up of several dioceses.

cooking iron: household cooking utensils of heavy cast iron similar to dutch ovens.

cooper: one who made and repaired wooden vessels formed of staves and hoops; a barrel maker.

co-parcenary: an estate held in common by joint heirs.

co-parcener: persons who have jointly inherited an estate by virtue of descent.

copeman: 1: a dishonest merchant, especially in horses. 2: a receiver of stolen goods.

coping: 1: the upper part of masonry or brickwork usually sloped. 2: the trimming or cutting of a hawk's beak or talons.

coping iron: an instrument used for cutting a hawk's beak or talons.

copperhead: during the Civil War, a northerner who was sympathetic with the Southern cause.

coppers: 1: a ship's cooking utensils. 2: a bronze or copper coin.

copyhold: the right by a written transcript or record to occupy a particular piece of land.

coqueluche: an epidemic of catarrh; later, of whooping-cough.

coram me: (*Lat.*) done by or in the presence of the person whose name follows.

cord: a measurement of wood, eight feet by four feet by four feet.

cord bed: a bed supported by cords tied at intervals between the side frames.

corder: a colonial official whose duty was to verify cords of wood before sale.

cordial: that which suddenly invigorates the system and stimulates the action of the heart or blood circulation; any medicine which increases strength or raises the spirits.

cordiner: variant of cordwainer.

cordon bleu: (*slang*) offspring of a black woman and a Frenchman.

corduroy road: a road made of tree trunks laid across a swampy area; bridges made in the same manner.

cordwainer: [*also* cordwainer] a shoemaker who worked in cordovan leathers.

cornage: a feudal form of rent determined by the number of horned cattle held by the tenant.

corn-cracker: (*slang*) a poor white in the South.

cornet: lowest grade of commissioned officer in calvary, whose duty was to carry the standard.

cornlaiters: (*obsolete*) a newly married couple who upheld the custom of begging corn to sow their first crop.

corporeal hereditament: tangible property that can be inherited.

corporeal right: a tangible right in property such as an estate.

corpse viewer: a coroner.

corpus: (*Lat.*) body; substance; flesh; corpse.

Corpus Christi: a moveable feast day in honor of the Eucharist.

correction house: (*Colonial American*) a facility to provide rehabilitation for the insane and petty lawbreakers.

corregidor: a principal town official in Spanish territory.

corruption: [*also* contagion] infected condition.

corruption of blood: (*Old English law*) the condition of a person who was disqualified from inheriting or transferring his estate to others because he was considered corrupt by treason or felony.

corse present: (*archaic*) 1: a mortuary, 2: a gift given to the clergy from the possessions of a householder at his death.

corserie: buying and selling; bartering.

corum: (*obsolete*) quorum.

cosin: (*obsolete*) cousin.

cosinage: (*obsolete*) cousinage.

costermonger: originally, a seller of apples; a fruiterer, especially in the open street.

coster-wife: a woman who sells fruit from an open stall in the street.

costiveness: constipation.

cot: 1: a small cottage. 2: a man who does housework usually done by a woman. 3: a child's bed.

cot-betty: a man who participates in the part of household affairs usually reserved for women.

coteller: the second vote counter in the House of Commons.

cotenancy: joint ownership or occupancy of land.

coterell: a cottar, a cottager.

coterie: an organized association or club.

coton: variant of cotton.

cotter: in the Domesday Book, one who lived in a cottage and worked a small piece of land (five acres) in return for service given to the lord.

cottonade: course cotton cloth.

cottondom: the Southern states.

cotton factor: one who buys and sells cotton.

cotton lord: a person who has become wealthy from the cotton industry.

cotton manies: those who work in cotton factories.

coucking stool: the stool upon which one was seated when in stocks.

coulee: a deep ravine caused by erosion and usually dry in the summer.

coulter: a heavy, knife-like part on the front of a plough for cutting soil.

councilor: an official member of the council of a colonial government such as a town, city, county, or district council.

counselor: 1: (*United States*) an attorney. 2: (*England*) a barrister; an advocate.

counter jumper: [*also* counter hopper] a clerk or shopkeeper's assistant.

counterpane: *see* coverlid.

country land: land which was granted to one of the New England colonies.

country mark: an identifying mark or scar put on a slave to show which part of Africa he/she came from.

country rate: tax assessment on the property of persons living in the New England colonies.

county home: [*also* county house] a poor house, where people who needed help were placed.

county orphans court: civil courts having jurisdiction over guardianships and adoptions.

county palatine: (*obsolete*) English dominion; territory of a count or earl.

county town: in England, a county seat.

coupe: a light four-wheeled carriage.

couper: one who barters, deals, or buys and sells.

coupon: (*United States*) a small ticket attached to certificates of State Stocks which drew interest.

coupon-clipper: (*slang*) a person of wealth.

couranteer: a journalist, reporter, or newspaper publisher.

coureur de bols: (*French*) [*also* courier] a hunter or trader who lived long periods in the wilderness and traded with the Indians.

courses and distances: *see* metes and bounds.

courtesy right: a husband's right to his wife's inherited estate.

court leet: a court of record held periodically and attended by the residents of the district.

Court of the Admiral: *see* Admiralty Court.

Court of Oyer and Terminer: a criminal court held in conjunction with the court of quarter sessions and usually heard by the same judges.

court week: the week a county court is in session.

cousin-german: first cousins.

cousin-red: kinship.

cove and key: [*also* closet and key; chamber and key] the functions and rights of the mistress of a house, from the age of fourteen or fifteen.

covenant: a formal agreement or promise in writing; a contract such as a deed.

covenant chain: a chain belt which symbolized peace between the colonists and the Indians.

covenantor: early Scotch-Irish Presbyterian immigrants—but not all who received the label actually were.

covenants of seisin: a covenant stating that the owner or grantor of an estate actually has the right to covey, and that he really is in possession of the estate.

coverlid: [*also* coverlet; counterpane] a woven bedspread.

coverture: the legal condition of a married woman which allows her to keep and control her personal property and wealth.

cowboy: Tory partisans of Westchester County, New York, who plundered and killed their opponents who favored the American cause.

cow-brute: a bull.

cow-common: [*also* cow-walk] community pasture; land common to all for grazing animals.

cowherd: a cow keeper; one who tends cows.

cowl: a large vessel for water, such as a tub.

cow lease: the right to pasture a cow in a cow-common, a pasture for the use of the inhabitants of a community.

cow-walk: *see* cow-common.

Coxey's Army: several hundred unemployed persons who marched to Washington under the leadership of J.S. Coxey in 1894 asking for legislative help.

coxswain: a helmsman of a boat having charge of the boat and crew.

cracker: 1: a back woodsman or border ruffian. 2: a poor white in the South.

cracker boy: a boy employed to clean and sort slate and other impurities from the coal crushed by the crackers (machines that crush anthracite coal).

cracky-wagon: a springless wagon drawn by one horse.

craftiman: a craftsman.

cramer: a peddler who sold books in the marketplace; a hawker.

cramp bark: bark of the American Cranberry tree, often used as an anti-spasmodic.

cramp colic: appendicitis.

creacure: (*obsolete*) [*also* creansour] creditor.

credit lands: public lands sold on credit.

creole: 1: a person of European descent (French or Spanish) born in Louisiana. 2: a black born in the western hemisphere, rather than Africa.

cresset: a vessel made to hold grease or oil, to be burnt for light, usually mounted on a pole or building, and often used for light on a wharf.

crest: a heraldic bearing or device used separately as an ornament or cognizance for plate, liveries, and the like which was worn on top of the helmet and is shown in that position on the achievement.

crew bonds: documents required of each master of a vessel as an assurance that, at the time of the vessel's return to a U.S. port, he would account for all persons named on a verified list that had been delivered to the collector of customs when the vessel departed from the United States.

crier: [*also* cryer] 1: a court officer. 2: a man appointed by a village to make announcements. 3: an auctioneer or hawker.

crimp: one who impresses (forcibly) men into the navy.

crocheteur: (obsolete) a porter.

croft: a small piece of ground, usually attached to a house, used for farming or pasture.

crofter: a tenant who works a small piece of ground, having another vocation, such as fishing.

crooked whisky: whisky on which the tax has not been paid nor a license issued.

cropper: a tenant who works a piece of ground and gets a portion of the crop in payment.

crop-sickness: sickness from an overextended stomach, usually from excess eating or drinking.

crossroads wedding: a marriage held at a crossroads after the sun had set, with the bride wearing only her shift (a type of slip worn under her clothing) to show that she had no debts to bring to the marriage.

croup: a disease known scientifically as acute obstructive laryngitis, diphtheria, or occasionally strep throat.

crouter: a person with Dutch or German heritage.

crowner: a coroner.

crownet: a coronet.

croze: a tool used by a cooper for making the groove in cask staves.

cryer: *see* crier.

crypt: a room or vault beneath a church.

cuckingstool: [*also* tumbrel; trebuchet] a machine or device used for punishing offenders by seating a person on the stool and immersing him or her in water.

cuffy: (*slang: nineteenth century*) [*also* cuffee] 1: a black in America. 2: a bear.

cuius susceptores: (*Lat.*) godparents

culler: formerly, a town official appointed to inspect fish.

culliver: (*obsolete*) a musket.

cum: (*Lat.*) with; along with; under; in; by.

Cumberland Road: *see* National Road.

cum onere: (*Lat.*) subject to a lien or obligation of which the buyer is aware.

cum testamento annexo: (*Lat.*) *literally* with the will annexed"; an administration of an estate where the will was made where either the executor was not named, did not qualify, or refused to serve.

cuppen: cow pen.

cupping: drawing blood using a cup from which the air has been removed.

curate: a deputy of a rector or vicar.

curation: guardianship over orphaned minors usually over the age of fourteen (male) and twelve (female) and under twenty-one.

curator: a guardian who was appointed to take care of a minor or incompetent person and to take care of their property.

cure: a parish priest in a French-speaking country.

curer: one who cures tobacco.

curia: the papal court.

Curia Regis Rolls: the minutes or proceedings of business conducted by the Crown.

curretter: (*obsolete*) a broker.

curricle: two-wheeled carriage pulled by two horses abreast.

currier: a craftsman who treats animal skins with oil or grease.

cursitor: English chancery court clerk whose duty is to draft original documents.

curtesy: under common law, a husband's fights to his wife's land at the time of her death.

curtilage: the grounds adjoining or surrounding a dwelling house.

curtle-ax: a cutlass.

cushion thumper: a Methodist preacher who indulges in animated actions during his sermon.

custodary: [*also* custodiary] a person or institution, such as a bank, having charge of public funds.

custom: a tax levied by the government on items brought into or carried out of the country.

customer: a customs collector.

custom house: a government office where customs are collected and paid.

cutler: one who makes, deals, and sharpens knives, scissors, and other cutting instruments.

Cutlerite: [*also* Gladdenite; Strangite; Brewsterite; Gatherite] a member of a sect broken from the Mormon church.

cut money: pieces of a coin which had been cut up into segments.

cut silver: silver money (dollar) cut into five quarters.

cyanosis: blueness of the skin due to lack of oxygen.

cyanotype: blueprint type paper used for photographs between 1855 and 1910.

cymytere: (*obsolete*) cemetery.

cynanche: diseases of the throat, characterized by inflammation, swelling, and difficulty breathing or swallowing.

cy pres: a rule whereby when it has become impossible, or impracticable to execute a will exactly as the testator wished, the courts will try to carry out his wishes "as near as possible."

cystitis: inflammation of the bladder.

cystotomy: the act of opening encysted tumors to discharge morbid matter.

D

daguerreotype: photographic process invented by L. J. M. Daguerre (1789-1857), a French painter, in which pictures were reproduced on silver plates by sensitizing them with iodine and then developing them with mercury.

dairy house: a barn or building used as a dairy; the home of a dairyman.

dairyman: a man who rented, owned, or managed a dairy and made his living by selling dairy products.

Dames of the Loyal Legion of the United States: organized in 1899 for women descendants of Union Army commissioned officers and wives of members of the Military Order of the Loyal Legion of the United States.

Damianists: a sect that denied any distinction of persons in the Godhead, believing in one single nature, yet calling God the Father, Son, and Holy Spirit.

damster: in logging operations, one who supervised the building of a dam.

dancing exercise: twitching and jerking induced in people by intense emotional excitement, aroused at revivalistic religious meetings.

dancing quaker: Shaker, called such because of intense emotional trembling and shaking.

danegeld: a tax levied annually to maintain forces to oppose the Danes or to buy them off.

dangue: *see* dengue.

dark-house: a madhouse or insane asylum.

dator: (*Lat.*) giver.

daturine: [*also* datura stramonium] a drug used to treat seizures and mental disorders.

Daughters of the American Revolution: *see* National Society of Daughters of the American Revolution.

Daughters of the Cincinnati: a group founded in 1894 for women descendants of the officers of George Washington's Continental Army or Navy.

Daughters of the Republic of Texas: a society founded in

1891 for women descendants of loyal Texans prior to annexation, 19 February 1846.

Daughters of Union Veterans of the Civil War, 1861-1865: a society incorporated in 1885 for women lineal descendants of soldiers and sailors of the Union Army, Navy, or Marine Corps who served honorably between 12 April 1861 and 9 April 1865.

day coach: a railroad car without sleeping provisions.

day fever: a fever of a day's duration or coming on in the daytime; the sweating sickness.

day laborer: a man who worked on a hire-by-the-day basis.

day-man: a day laborer.

de: (*Lat.*) from; out of; about; at; for.

dead house: a place where bodies were kept while waiting for burial.

dean and chapter: the legal corporation of a church in which the dean heads an assembly or group of members called a chapter.

de anno in annum: (*Lat.*) from year to year.

deathsman: an executioner.

de avo: (*Lat.*) from the grandfather.

debarred: the condition of a person who, for some reason, is no longer allowed to serve in an official or public office.

de bene esse: something done out of normal sequence; for example, evidence given before a trial for fear it would be lost due to age, infirmity, or the impending death of the person giving the evidence.

debet et detinet: (*Lat.*) he owes and detains.

de bonis non: (*Lat.*) *literally* "of the goods not administered"; the distribution of property not completed by the first administrator.

de bonis non cum: (*Lat.*) *see* de bonis non; but with the will attached.

de bono et male: (*Lat.*) for good and ill.

decalogue: the Ten Commandments collectively as a body of law.

decedent: a deceased person.

decessit: (*Lat.*) died.

decessit sine parole: (*Lat.*) died without issue.

decessit vita patria: (*Lat.*) died in father's lifetime.

decido: (*Lat.*) to die.

de clamo: (*Lat.*) of a claim.

decree pro confessee: (*Lat.*) judgment because of confessions.

decree of distribution: [*also* assignment of real estate] the final document issued in a probate case which tells how the estate was distributed and by what relationship the heirs received title to the property.

decrepitude: a state of feebleness and decay due to old age.

de die in diem: (*Lat.*) from day to day.

de denis: (*Lat.*) of gifts.

deed of acquittance: a deed by which additional acreage is transferred or sold to the original patent owner when and if it was found that, by survey, the patented land had more acreage than was originally thought.

deed of agreement: a deed concerned with the sale of personal property, deeds land to persons who agree to take care of the grantor for the remainder of his life.

deed of conveyance: document showing the transfer of ownership of property and perhaps the ownership of a land warrant.

deed of decree: document showing property transferred usually as a result of a petition or court action.

deed of gift: deed showing a transfer of property made without a monetary payment as consideration.

deed of separation: an instrument through the medium of a third party acting as trustee, in which provision is made by a husband for separation from his wife, and for her separate maintenance.

deed of trust: a mortgage arrangement which allows a third party to hold the deed until the buyer has paid his debt.

deed poll: a deed made by one person, and only one person is obligated to fulfill the terms of the deed.

deemster: a judge; *(Scotland)* the officer of a court who pronounces sentence as directed by the judge.

de facto: (*Lat.*) *literally* "in fact"; something accomplished and done but not necessarily legally sanctioned.

defeasance: a collateral deed which, upon certain conditions, will make another deed null and void.

Defenders of Baltimore: *see* General Society of the War of 1812.

degener: (*Lat.*) low-born or base.

degrade: adverse wind or bad weather causing delay in a journey.

degree of consanguinity: degree of blood relationship used to determine right of inheritance.

degree of relationship: the distance between two persons related by blood—under Canon Law (used in most states) two persons who descend from a common ancestor, but not one from the other (brothers, cousins, etc.) have collateral consanguinity and a degree of relationship of the same number as the number of generations the furthest is removed from the closest common progenitor: for example, an uncle and nephew are related in the second degree because the nephew is two generations from the common ancestor (his grandfather and his uncle's father). Two brothers are related in the first degree and first cousins are related to each other in the second degree, and so on. In lineal relationships (direct line) each generation is a degree.

de jure: (*Lat.*) *literally* "by right"; an action or deed lawfully and legitimately accomplished as opposed to de facto.

delaine: a light wool, or wool and cotton, dress fabric.

delirium tremens: [*also* delirium tremors; DTs] a condition found in persons whose use of alcohol is excessive resulting in hallucinations, both visual and auditory.

demesne: land possessed by a lord and used by him rather than rented out to tenants.

demurrer: a delay or stay; a document filed in a case by the defendant asking the court not to accept the plaintiff's declaration even if true, as sufficient evidence to support a judgment in behalf of the plaintiff.

denaturalization: the process of withdrawing previously granted citizenship, due to fraud or other illegal acts on the part of the alien.

demihag: [*also* demihake; demihaque; half-haque; half-hagg] a long pistol used in the sixteenth century.

demijohn: a glass or stoneware bottle, with a thin neck, holding approximately ten gallons.

demise: a transfer of property when it is leased for a specified number of years.

dengue: [*also* dangue] an acute infectious fever, characterized by excruciating pain in the joints but seldom proving fatal, which is epidemic and sporadic in East Africa and the countries surrounding the Indian Ocean.

denicalis: (*Lat.*) a ceremony of purification which takes place ten days after a person's death.

democrat: [*also* democratic wagon] a light four-wheeled cart with several seats one behind the other pulled by two horses.

demurrage: money paid to the master of a trading vessel for delay or detention in port beyond the appointed departure time.

denization: [*also* denizenship] the act of giving a degree of citizenship or partial citizenship to an alien and giving the person the fight to buy and sell property but not to vote or hold office.

denizen: a person with certain limited citizenship rights; one who obtained letters patent from the King making him a subject.

denizenship: *see* denization.

denomino: (*Lat.*) to name; to call.

de novo: (*Lat.*) completely new from the start.

dentition: cutting of the teeth.

denubo: (*Lat.*) to marry; to marry beneath one's station.

de parte domus: (*Lat.*) of part of the house.

departer: (*nineteenth century*) a gold or silver refiner.

de partition facienda: (*Lat.*) a writ that allows a sheriff to partition or divide lands.

deplumation: (*nineteenth century*) a tumor of the eyelids which results in loss of hair.

deported alien: an alien considered dangerous, who was deported under the Alien Act of 1798 (the act died two yeas later).

Descendants of the Illegitimate Sons and Daughters of the Kings of Britain: a society organized in 1950 by four fellows of the American Society of Genealogists for men and women who can prove descent from an illegitimate son, daughter, grandson, or granddaughter of a King or Queen of England, Scotland, or Wales.

Descendants of the New Jersey Settlers: a group organized in 1940 by descendants of the King, Swayze, Thomas, Farrar, Cory, and Horton families in Mississippi whose ancestors, between 1772 and 1775, emigrated from New Jersey to the Old Natchez District, settling on the Ogden Mandamus.

Descendants of the Signers of the Declaration of Independence: a group founded in 1907 for any lineal descendant (adults and juniors) of a signer of the Declaration of Independence.

de son tort: (*Lat.*) of his own wrong; having no authority to act.

destrere: (*obsolete*) a war-horse or charger.

de tempore in tempus: (*Lat.*) from time to time.

detinue: a common law action to recover or obtain compensation for personal property that has been illegally detained.

detur: (*Lat.*) let there be given.

devastavit: a writ against a person acting as executor or administrator of an estate for acts of waste, omission, or mismanagement of the estate.

de ventre inspiciendo: (*Lat.*) *literally* "of examining the abdomen"; a writ issued by a presumptive heir-at-law who wished to find out if a widow was pregnant.

devil: a junior legal counsel who does work usually without pay; a person hired by another, such as an author, to do parts of his work without recognition and under the author's name.

devisavit vel non: (*Lat.*) whether the paper propounded is, or is not, the last will and testament of the deceased.

devise: to give real property by will.

devisee: the person to whom real property is left in a will.

devisor: a person (the testator) who leaves real property to another by will.

devolution: the passing of property, title, legal rights, or interests to another by legal processes.

dey: (*obsolete*) a woman in charge of a dairy; a female servant.

dey-wife: a dairywoman.

diaphoretic: a medicine or preparation that induces perspiration.

diary fever: a fever that lasts one day.

dicker: a number or lot of ten— a dicker of hides, or gloves.

dico: (*Lat.*) to tell; to order; to plead.

died without issue: died without having children.

dies: (*Lat.*) day; daylight; day of burial.

dies palmarum: [*also* Dominica ad Palmas] a moveable feast day, Palm Sunday, the sixth Sunday in Lent.

diet-drink: medicated liquors or drink prepared with medicinal ingredients.

digitalis: a medicine used as a heart stimulant, prepared from the fox-glove.

dike-grave: English officer in charge of drains, sluices, and sea-banks in a specific area under the Court of Sewers.

diker: one who builds dikes or digs ditches or trenches.

diligence: a warrant for the attachment of a person's lands or effects for security of a debt.

dingy: [*also* dinghey; dinghy] a small rowboat.

diphtheria: a contagious throat disease characterized by the formation of a false membrane in the air passages.

diptych: a public register, so called because it consisted of two hinged leaves folded together.

direct tax: a tax of any one of three types: personal property tax, real property (real estate) tax, and poll or head tax.

dirk cane: a cane containing a short, straight dagger, known as a dirk—this was a taxable item in 1860.

discidium: (*Lat.*) separation; divorce.

discovert: an unmarried woman or widow; a woman not under protection of a husband.

discretionary trust: power given to a trustee to use his own judgment in caring for the lands, investments, or funds of another person.

disend: a rough sketch map of Spanish and Mexican land grants in California, contained in the case files (expedientes).

dismarry: to annul a marriage.

dismission: discharge by the court of an executor or administrator who has completed his duties in regard to an estate's administration.

disownment: in church records, one who has been terminated from church membership for disciplinary reasons.

dispensation: a special release from obligation.

dispepsia: *see* dyspepsia.

displayed: in heraldry, wings extended, of birds of prey.

dispone: to assign, make over, or grant; to convey land.

disposal: the sale of public land by the federal government to private parties.

disposition: a deed of conveyance of property.

disseisin: the state of being illegally and forcefully removed from one's lands or property; *(pre-fifteenth century)* the state of being removed from one's lands or one's moveable goods.

distaff: in heraldry, a symbol used to denote the female sex, the type of work a woman does, female authority, or a female heir—the spindle-side represents the female side of the family, and the spear-side represents the male.

distributee: one who is entitled to part of an estate that is being distributed.

distiller: one who makes alcoholic beverages.

distrain: the act of lawfully or unlawfully seizing personal property to compel someone to perform on an official obligation such as appear in court, pay rent, etc.

distraint: an official action, ordered by the court, consisting of the seizure of property to force a person to appear in court or cause them to make payment of unpaid taxes.

distress: to hold the property of another after it has been distrained. *See* distrain.

District of West Augusta: located in what is now the southwest corner of Pennsylvania, south of the Ohio, Allegheny, and Kiskiminetas Rivers and the northern portion of West Virginia, between the Maryland state line on the east and the Ohio River on the West.

dittybag: a bag carried by sailors in which to store their smaller personal possessions.

diurnal: a journal or diary; a record of daily happenings published every day.

diversory: a temporary lodging place such as an inn.

divident: land divided and included in a patent or grant.

divider: a man whose duty it was to divide an estate equally among the heirs.

doarium: (*obsolete*) dower.

dock fever: yellow fever.

dock-walloper: a laborer working on docks and wharfs.

dog-day: the days between the last part of July and the first part of September, when Sirius, or the dog star, rises and sets with the sun.

dogger: a Dutch fishing vessel used in herring fishery, similar to a yawl.

dog leg: a fence made laying logs or trees horizontally on supports crossed in the shape of an "x."

dog leech: a veterinarian.

Dohrman's Grant: established in 1801 and located half in Tuscarawas County and half in Harrison County, Ohio.

dole: money or food distributed to the poor.

domescart: the executioner's cart.

Domesday Book: [also Doomesday Book] ancient record of the Grand or Great Inquest or Survey of lands in England by the order of William the Conqueror, giving a census-like description of the realm, with the names of the propri-etors and the nature, extent, value, liabilities, etc., of their properties.

domesman: a judge.

domestic: 1: a sister, female relative, or female servant (not necessarily related to the head of a household) who lived with a family and helped with the housework. 2: [also cotton do-mestic] unbleached muslin type cloth—domestic as opposed to imported.

domina: (Lat.) mistress of a family; lady; wife.

domine: (Lat.) [also dominie] Lord or master; used as a form of address when speaking to clergy or members of learned professions.

Dominica ad Palmas: see dies palmarum.

Dominica Rogationum: a moveable feast day, Rogation Sunday, the fifth Sunday after Easter.

dominicum: (Lat.) absolute ownership or inheritance.

dominie: a preacher. See domine.

dominion: feudal lands or do-mains of a lord.

dominus: (Lat.) master of the house; owner; ruler.

domus: (Lat.) house; home; family; native country.

donatio: (Lat.) a gift or dona-tion.

donatio inter vivos: (Lat.) a gift among living persons.

donatio mortis causa: (Lat.) gift in prospect of death.

donation land: public lands donated or given to settlers for fulfilling certain requirements, generally in exchange for military service.

donation tract: donation land grants given in 1792 and situated in Washington and Morgan counties in Ohio.

donative: a parish exempt from jurisdiction of the bishop of the diocese.

donee: one who receives a gift or trust without first giving consideration; a person to whom lands are given entail.

doomage: a tax levied by town officials for non-payment of fees on taxable property; the officials doom (judge) and set the tax at their discretion.

Doomesday Book: *see* Domesday Book,

door-keeper: a janitor, porter, or guard.

doquet: (*nineteenth century*) a warrant or paper granting particular license.

dorse: the back of a document or page containing additional information; endorsement.

dos rationabilis: (*Lat.*) reasonable dower.

dotalis: (*Lat.*) dower.

double assessment: a fine for failure to report property owned.

doughface: a Northern politician who favored the South in the matter of slavery.

dowager: a widow with a title or rank—the queen dowager; a jointure, or property from her husband.

dower: provision made from a husband's estate for the support of his widow and family, usually one third of the value of the estate (real estate only).

dower chest: a wooden chest, used along the same lines as a hope chest.

dower release: an agreement which forfeited a wife's right to any of her deceased husband's land (dower) that he had sold to another—in some cases a widow was able to reclaim land that her husband had acquired in fee simple and subsequently sold, even 50 years after the sale, unless the buyer had acquired a dower release from the owner's wife. *See* dower; dower right; fee simple.

dower right: the right of a wife to one-third of the land which her husband had at the time of their marriage or acquired during the marriage, after his death.

dowery: [*also* dowry] any land, money, goods, or personal property brought by a bride to her husband in marriage.

dowlas: [*also* dowles] heavy linen made in England.

dowry: *see* dowery.

dowser: a water-diviner; one who makes use of a divining rod to find water.

dowsing rod: the divided rod or stick used by a dowser.

doxy: the unmarried mistress of a beggar or rogue.

drachm: unit of weight with several different values, frequently a dram.

drachma: basic monetary unit in Greece, equal to a few cents U.S. money.

dragoon: heavily armed, mounted infantryman.

dram: 1/8 of a fluid ounce.

draper: originally a maker of woolen cloth, later a dealer in cloths of all kinds.

Draper Manuscripts: Lyman Copeland Draper's (1815-91) collection of manuscript documents (correspondence, interviews, newspaper extracts, muster rolls, etc.) which cover the period from 1755 to 1815 in the western Carolinas, Virginia, Georgia, Alabama, the entire Ohio River Valley, and parts of the Mississippi River Valley.

draught: land which had been surveyed and draughted, for which settlers drew lots. 2: a drink, specifically for those who were ill, made of eggs and milk.

draught horse: a work horse.

drawer: one who drew and served liquor for tavern customers.

draw knife: a knife with a handle on each end used for scraping.

draw-latch: a sneak thief.

draw shave: a drawing-knife used for shaving spokes, table legs, etc.

dray: a vehicle, such as a sled or cart, without wheels, used for dragging wood, turf, etc.

drayage: the fee charged for hauling goods by dray.

drayhorse: a large, powerful horse used to pull a dray.

drayman: one who drives a dray, often used in connection with a brewery.

dreng: a free tenant who held tenure that was older than the Norman conquest, which was partly military, partly servile.

dresser: one who dresses another (a tirewoman). 2: a surgeon's assistant in a hospital.

driver: the overseer of a group of slaves.

dropsy: an abnormal collection of fluid in the tissues and cavities of the body.

dropsy of the brain: (*obsolete*) encephalitis. *See* hydrocephalus.

drover: a driver of sheep and cattle.

drugger: a druggist.

drummer: a commercial traveler or salesman who sometimes used a drum to attract attention to his wares.

dry bellyache: [*also* dry dripes] lead poisoning.

drysalter: one who deals in salted or dried meats, pickles, sauces, chemical, and dyes.

duces tecum: (*Lat.*) bring with you.

duchess: the wife or widow of a duke; a woman who holds the position of a duke in her own right.

ducking stool: a seat on the end of a long pole where one was tied and held out over water for ducking.

ducking tumbrel: a ducking stool with wheels.

duco: (*Lat.*) to marry; to take; to bring.

due bill: a written certificate much like a promissory note.

duffer: a peddler or hawker who sells cheap or trashy goods. 2: something of little value.

dum sola: (*Lat.*) while unmarried.

dung: animal manure.

dungaree: a coarse, inferior Indian calico.

Dunkers: [*also* Dunkards] German-American Baptists who administer baptism only to adults by dunking them three times. *See* Brethren church.

duplicem valorem maritagii: (*Lat.*) double the value of the marriage.

durante minore aetate: (*Lat.*) during minority.

durante vidiutate: (*Lat.*) during widowhood.

durham boat: a long keel boat, resembling an Indian canoe, used on east coast rivers in the United States

dustman: a janitor or garbageman.

dustyfoot: a traveling peddler.

Dutch Settlers Society of Albany: a society founded in 1924 for adults descended from a person who resided in Fort Orange resident (the Colony of Rensselaerswyck), and the Village of Beverwyck before 1665.

Dutch West Indies Company: a company formed by the Netherlands to secure their claim to lands in North America in 1621. The first families were brought out by the company in 1623 and in 1626, where they founded New Amsterdam.

dux: (*Lat.*) leader; guide.

duxit: (*Lat.*) married; husband.

dys: prefixed to medical terms, means painful, impaired, or irregular.

dyscrasy: an ill habit or state of the bodily humors; an abnormal condition of the body.

dysorexy: a diminished appetite.

dyspepsia: [*also* dispepsia] bad digestion usually involving weakness, loss of appetite, and depression.

dysury: difficulty in discharging urine, accompanied by pain and a sensation of heat.

E

eadem: (*Lat.*) in the same way.

eagle: (*nineteenth century*) a ten dollar gold coin in use in the United States.

eald: (*obsolete*) old.

ealdren: (*obsolete*) for elder.

eam: (*obsolete*) uncle.

ear: to plough or turn up the ground.

earer: a ploughman.

earike: a fine or tax paid for an amount of ground ploughed.

earth: a day's ploughing.

earth-bath: a medical treatment in which the patient was buried up to the shoulders in the ground.

earth stopper: a person employed to "stop up" fox holes.

easement: a right to use another's land because of necessity or convenience.

easement appurtenant: a n easement proper or one which passes with the dominant estate to all subsequent grantees and is inheritable.

easement in gross: a personal privilege to use another's land, which is not assignable and cannot be inherited.

easement of necessity: an easement necessary for the continued use of land when a large tract has been subdivided.

Easter Even: the day between Good Friday and Easter Day.

Eastertide: the weeks following Easter Day and leading to Ascension Day.

eatage: (*obsolete*) the right to use a pasture for grazing, especially the growth after the hay is cut.

Eaton Code: a code of biblical interpretation published in London in 1657, and required reading for each household in New Haven, Connecticut.

Ebenezer Society: *see* Amana Church Society.

ecclesia: (*Lat.*) church.

eclampsy: 1: a symptom of epilepsy. 2: convulsions during pregnancy.

ecstasy: in medicine, a species of catalepsy, wherein reason is temporarily suspended.

edema: nephrosis; a swelling of tissues.

edema of lungs: congestive heart failure or a form of dropsy.

edematous: swelling with a serous humor; dropsical.

edge leam: an edge tool.

editicius: (*Lat.*) named; allowed.

edom die: (*Lat.*) indicating same place, same day.

eel thing: (*obsolete*) St. Anthony's fire.

eggler: a person who deals in eggs and poultry.

ego: (*Lat.*) I; I myself.

eight-br: (*Old Style calendar*) [*also* 8br] October.

eir: (*obsolete*) [*also* eire] heir.

ejectment: in common law, a lawsuit brought against an intruder by the person leasing the land; later, a means of finding if the owner had valid title by producing a fictitious lessee to test it in court.

ejus: (*Lat.*) his; hers; of him.

eld: legal or full age; old age.

elderne: elderly or old.

eld father: a grandfather.

eld mother: a grandmother.

election court: a seventeenth-century court in colonial New England which met to elect the officials of the colonies.

eleemosynary: alms given to the church; a charitable gift or donation.

elephantiasis: a species of leprosy, so called from the skin being covered with incrustations, marked by a thickening and greasiness of the legs, loss of hair and feeling, swelling of the face, and a hoarse nasal voice.

eleven-penny bit: [*also* York Shilling; Spanish Real] a coin commonly in use in colonial New York and Pennsylvania.

elixir: a drug or medicine supposed to have the power to prolong life; cure-all; eventually, quack medicine.

ell: a measure of a length of cloth, about forty-five inches.

elsen: an awl used by a shoemaker.

elugeo: (*Lat.*) to mourn the full time.

emancipated child: a child who has reached the legal age to be free from his parents' control, and having the right to keep his own earnings and purchase property under his own name.

emblement: a crop grown and produced by the labor and industry of a tenant, which legally belongs to the tenant.

eminent domain: the right of the government to condemn or take over private property for public use.

emorior: (*Lat.*) to die; to perish; to cease.

emporium: a trading center or market place.

Empresario: a man who performed a specific deed, such as importing a certain number of settlers, in return for land grants and power.

emptor: a buyer.

en auter droit: in another's right.

encephalitis: swelling of the brain caused by inflammation following an infectious disease—often called sleeping sickness, but not to be confused with African sleeping sickness.

endow: to give a dowery, or income, for support of an institution or of a widow—who was endowed with a part of her husband's estate. *See* dower.

enfeoff: to create a feoffment or to convey freehold estates.

engendrure: generation; parentage; descent; origin.

engross: the use of a large clear hand to write or transcribe; the prescribed method for preparing an official document.

entail: to put a restriction on how land could be passed on to descendants.

entailed estate: an estate limited in the manner that it can be transferred, such as allowing the estate to be inherited only by a specific line of heirs, and preventing one from transferring it outside of that line.

entailment: a limitation or interference with the regular process of inheritance.

entailment: inheritance limited to a specific succession of heirs.

enteric fever: typhoid fever.

enterocolitis: an inflammation affecting both the small and large intestine.

enteritis: inflammation of the bowels—usually acute rather than chronic.

entirety: similar to joint tenancy, where one or more own the whole of the land.

entry taker: local (county) court appointed official.

enubo: (*Lat.*) to marry out of one's rank; to marry and leave the paternal house.

enuptio: (*Lat.*) marrying out of one's rank.

enutrio: (*Lat.*) to nourish; to bring up.

eodem: (*Lat.*) to the same place; just so far.

eodem die: (*Lat.*) same day.

Ephiphania Domini: (*Lat.*) a fixed feast day, Epiphany.

epigraph: an inscription on a building or mausoleum.

epistaxis: a nose bleed.

epitaphuim: (*Lat.*) funeral oration.

epithelial: of or pertaining to epithelium, cancerous cells.

equitable ownership: the state of receiving the benefits or use of real estate without actually being the owner named on the deed—for example, when a trust is set up, the trustee is the legal owner, while the beneficiary is the equitable owner.

equitable title: the right to a legal title upon fulfilling certain circumstances, such as paying off a mortgage.

equity of redemption: the law which allows one, whose property is in the process of foreclosure, to regain his/her land by paying the mortgage in full plus the costs of foreclosure.

eremite: a hermit or recluse.

ergo: (*Lat.*) therefore.

erite: a heretic.

erratum: (*Lat.*) error, mistake.

erysipelas: [*also* Saint Anthony's Fire] a skin disease caused by strep infection which devastates the blood.

escheat: land that reverts back to the state or the Crown because no proven heirs could be found.

escrow: a document, instrument, or payment held by a third party and delivered when the conditions of an agreement are met.

espouse: a bride or bridegroom; a betrothed person of either sex.

esquire: a title of courtesy; a candidate for knighthood; a person of great wealth or influence.

essence peddler: one who sold medicines, flavorings, elixirs, etc.

estafette: a mounted messenger or courier.

estate at will: *see* estate from year to year.

estate for years: an estate based on a lease, valid for a definite and specified period of time, and bound by a contract in which payment or rent is established.

estate from year to year: [*also* estate at will] an estate which extends for an unspecified period of time, and renewed at regular intervals, based on an agreement between the parties.

estate sale: the sale of a deceased person's property to settle the estate, usually conducted by the executor or administrator.

estate tail: an estate with a special condition attached to it, such as it can only be inherited by the direct issue in the male or in the female line.

estoil: a heraldic charge in the form of a five-pointed star with wavy points or rays.

estray books: a record of missing livestock.

estreat: a true copy or extract of an original written document for use in a court.

et: (*Lat.*) and; also; yet.

et al: (*Lat.*) and others.

et uxor: (*Lat.*) and wife.

Eucharist: 1: (*from Greek*) giving of thanks. 2: universally, Holy Communion.

evito: (*Lat.*) to kill.

ex, e: a prefix, before consonants indicating out of, from, down from, after, etc.

ex asse heres: (*Lat.*) universal or sole heir.

ex assensu patris: (*Lat.*) by assent of the father.

Exaud: a moveable feast day, the sixth Sunday after Easter.

Exchequer Court: English court having jurisdiction over matters relating to the American colonies, which also issued licenses to go abroad.

Exchequer Roll: a record of rents and fines collected by sheriffs.

exciseman: a government official who collects excises (taxes).

excise tax: any duty, toll, or tax; a tax on imported goods.

ex contractu: (*Lat.*) by way of contract.

excrescence: an unnatural or disfiguring outgrowth of the skin.

ex curia: (*Lat.*) out of court.

executor: the individual appointed by the one making the will to dispose of his or her property after death in accordance with the terms of the will.

executor deed: *see* administrator deed

ex donationes regis: (*Lat.*) by gift of the king.

execessus: (*Lat.*) departure; death.

executor de son tort: one who illegally takes over for his own use, a deceased person's personal property when the estate has no legal representative.

executor nominate: an executor named by the testator; items exempt from sale after the death of the owner to clear his debts, such as furniture, tools, clothes, etc. which will allow the widow to support herself.

exeo: (*Lat.*) to go out or away.

exequy: (*Lat.*) funeral rites or ceremony.

ex facto: (*Lat.*) from or by the deed.

exheres: (*Lat.*) disinherited.

ex officio: (*Lat.*) by virtue of office.

exorior: (*Lat.*) to arise; to begin; to originate.

ex parte: (*Lat.*) judicial proceeding or judgment brought on behalf of one party without notifying the other party.

ex parte paterna: (*Lat.*) by the father's side.

expatriate: one deported from one's native land.

expede: to sign, seal, and deliver a document.

expediente: a case file written in Spanish regarding private land claims in California, verifying claims based on Spanish or Mexican grants.

ex post facto: (*Lat.*) after the act.

ex rel: (*Lat.*) upon the relation of.

exscribo: (*Lat.*) to write off; to copy.

exsequialis: (*Lat.*) funeral.

exspiro: (*Lat.*) to breathe out; to exhale; to die; to cease.

extant: (*Lat.*) in existence or not destroyed.

ex testamento: (*Lat.*) in accordance with the treatment of.

extravasated blood: ruptured blood vessel.

Extreme Unction: anointing with oil in case of death or imminent death.

F

faber: artisan; workman; smith; carpenter.

fabricator: (*Lat.*) artificer; maker; framer.

factor: a commissioned agent; one who sells goods for another in his own name and receives a commission.

faculty: a person who did not own land and was a professional, and thus was taxed on income—faculty included lawyers, physicians, dentists, carpenters, merchants, bankers, etc.

fagot: 1: a bundle of sticks or iron. 2: a person hired to take the place of another in roll call or muster.

failure of issue: in a will or deed, indicates that in the event of there being no children born to or surviving the deceased person, the property will go to a third party; in common law, the condition continues with the children of the first taker.

Fairfax Proprietary: *see* Northern Neck

faldstool: a portable folding seat used by a bishop when visiting other churches; a portable stool or desk used in praying.

fallow: land which is plowed but not sown to enrich the soil.

famula: (*Lat.*) female slave; maid-servant.

famulary: (*Lat.*) of or belonging to servants.

famulate: (*Lat.*) to be a servant.

fancy man: a man who lives upon the earnings of a prostitute; a pimp.

fancy woman: a mistress or a prostitute.

fanega: a Spanish bushel (two and one-half bushels).

fanner: one who winnows (separates and the chaff from the grain by means of air movement) grain with a fan.

fanning mill: a blower or fan for removing chaff, husks, dirt, etc., from grain.

farandman: a stranger or traveler, especially a traveling merchant.

farmed out: to contract with an institution, another family, etc. for the maintenance and care of persons at a prearranged price.

farmer: one who undertakes the collection of taxes or revenues; one who rents or has a lease of anything.

farrier: a blacksmith or horseshoer.

farthing: a fourth of a British penny. 2: an English measure of land equaling thirty acres.

farthingale: a hoop made of whalebone used for women's petticoats and skirts popular in the sixteenth and seventeenth centuries.

farthingdeal: an English measurement equaling one-fourth of an acre.

fashioner: one who fashions or forms anything, especially clothing.

fast estate: see realty.

father-in-law: often, a stepfather.

fathom: a measurement the length of outstretched arms or six feet.

fawkenere: (*obsolete*) [*also* fawkner] English for a falconer; one who breeds and trains falcons.

fealty: loyalty or fidelity owed to a feudal lord by his tenant.

feather merchant: a person who did not contribute by work or service in time of war.

febrifuge: any substance such as a plant, root, or herb that reduces fever.

febrile: being feverish or having a high temperature.

Federalist: a member of the Federalist political party supporting a strong central government.

fee: an estate, completely owned by a person, which can be sold or given as an inheritance by that person; an estate held by a lord to be given when service has been performed or homage paid.

feeder: 1: a servant or one who is supported by his lord. 2: a herdsman.

fee simple: an inheritance having no conditions or limitations in its use; a direct and complete inheritance.

fee simple absolute: an estate with no limitations or conditions.

fee tail: an estate limited in the manner that it can be passed on to heirs; property that cannot be sold but only transferred by inheritance.

feet of fines: documents, first kept during the reign of Richard I, that had the same function as deeds in transferring land; the bottom part of an indenture or deed kept by the recording office.

feller: a woodcutter.

fellmonger: a dealer in animal skins and hides, especially sheepskin.

felon: 1: an infection on the end of a finger or toe. 2: a criminal.

felony: (*feudal system*) an offense committed by a vassal for which he had to surrender his fief as punishment.

feme: (*Lat.*) a woman or wife.

feme-covert: a married woman dependant on and under protection of her husband having no legal rights to inherit, sell or buy property.

feme sole: an unmarried woman or a married woman independent of her husband with respect to property.

feme sole trader: a free trader, a married woman who holds property independently of her husband and is empowered by court action to buy, sell, or trade property on her own.

femina: (*Lat.*) female, woman.

femme de chambre: a chamber maid; a lady's maid.

fen: 1: a fee, or feudal benefice. 2: a tenure where the vassal, in place of military service, makes a return in grain or in money; a grant of land to be so held.

fence viewer: one who has charge of inspecting, locating, and erecting fences in a certain district.

fen-duty: a land tax.

feod: an estate held under a feudal lord.

feodary: *see* feudary.

feoffment: the means of conveying title to freehold estates in medieval England, requiring the livery of seisin (a ceremony where the person selling property would stand at the site in the presence of neighboring tenants and point out the boundaries to the purchaser. The seller would then hand to the buyer the symbol of seisin, often a twig and clump of earth from the land purchased, to bind the agreement.

fermacy: (*obsolete*) a pharmacy.

fermerere: (*obsolete*) 1: the person in charge of the infirmary in a monastery. 2: a farmer.

ferramentum: (*Lat.*) any tool, especially one used in agriculture.

ferrer: 1: a smith who works in iron. 2: one who has charge of the horses in a large household.

ferriage: the business of ferrying persons; the fare to be paid.

ferrotype: [*also* tintype] an Ambrotype photographic process using thin metal, popular from 1855 to 1900, resulting in black, deep gray, or chocolate brown positive images on piece of japanned iron.

Festum Eucharistie: a moveable feast day, the Thursday before Easter.

Festum Omnium Sanctorum: a fixed feast day, All Saints, the first of November.

feud: land granted by a feudal lord to a tenant on condition of services to be performed.

feudary: [*also* feodary; feudatory] a vassal or feudal tenant.

feudum evitum: ancestral fee.

fever: blacksmith.

fever powder: a remedy for subduing or curing fever.

fewterer: (*obsolete*) one who tends to greyhounds; an attendant.

fiduciary: an individual such as a guardian, executor, agent, administrator, attorney, conservator, or trustee empowered to act for the benefit of another.

filer: something over which one has rights or executes control; originally, the land held under feudal law on condition of rendering services.

field: in heraldry, the surface or part of the surface of a shield on which the charges or figures are arranged.

field driver: an officer in charge of catching stray animals and confining them.

figure flinger: an astrologer.

filia: (*Lat.*) daughter, female offspring.

filia fratris: (*Lat.*) brother's daughter (niece).

filia sororis: (*Lat.*) sister's daughter (niece).

filibuster: an irregular American soldier who promoted rebellions in Latin America; *(Southwest frontier)* a member of a motley assortment of con men, cutthroats, and some idealists who tried to take Texas from Mexico and Spain.

filii nobelium: (*Lat.*) sons of nobles.

filiola: (*Lat.*) little daughter.

filiolus: (*Lat.*) little son.

filius: (*Lat.*) son; male offspring.

filius fratris: (*Lat.*) brother's son; nephew.

filius nullius: (*Lat.*) an illegitimate person.

filius populi: (*Lat.*) *literally "a son of the people"*; a bastard.

filius sororis: (*Lat.*) sister's son; nephew.

final papers: *see* second papers.

fip: a fippenny bit, one-half of a bit or one-half of a Spanish Real; one-sixteenth of a coin or one-sixteenth of a dollar taken in silver coin.

firearms license: a written document giving permission to have firearms on one's possession, the contents of which included name, residence, and description of firearms.

Fire Lands: [*also* Ohio Land Grants, 1792] lands granted by Connecticut in 1792, to persons who suffered because of fires by the English during the Revolutionary War, particularly at New London, Fairfield, and Norwalk.

firkin: a measurement equal to one-fourth of a barrel.

fish fag: a woman who sells fish.

fistula: 1: an abnormal passage from an abscess or cavity to the skin or to another abscess. 2: a gold or silver tube through which the communicants received the sacrament.

fistulator: (*Lat.*) one who plays a reed-pipe.

fitter: a coal broker who represents a particular mine.

five civilized tribes: the five Indian tribes considered to be the most civilized: the Cherokee, Chickasaw, Choctaw, Creek, and Seminole.

fixture: chattel or goods attached to a house that go with it when sold.

flagon: a large pitcher-shaped vessel usually made of precious metal.

Flagon and Trencher: Descendants of Colonial Tavern Keepers: a group established in 1962 for adult descendants of persons keeping a tavern, inn, ordinary, etc., prior to 4 July 1776.

flail: a tool with a free-swinging stick (a swiple or swingle) tied to another stick and used by farmers to thresh grain.

flathead: a Chinook Indian.

fleam: [*also* phlebotomia] surgical knife used for opening veins for letting blood.

flesher: 1: a butcher. 2: one who works in a tannery.

flesh fork: a fork used for lifting meat into a pot.

fleshing knife: a tool used by a tanner to scrape the hair off hides.

flesh mark: marks such as cuts, slits, or holes in the ears, or brands made to identify livestock.

fleshmonger: one who deals in flesh; a pimp.

fletcher: a maker of and dealer in bows and arrows.

float: a certificate issued by the federal government to Indians for acquired lands.

Floreal: in the Republican Calendar, the month of blossoms.

florruit: (*Lat.*) he flourished.

Flotilla Service: organized during the War of 1812 against Britain, the first organization of the U.S. Army with which the Sea Fencibles protected ports, harbors, and the coast.

flourished: the condition of being alive at a certain time, although the exact dates are not known.

flummery: a food with a jelly-like substance made of flour and oatmeal.

flux: the drainage or discharge of liquid from a body cavity.

flux of humor: circulation.

fogger: 1: a peddler who carries small wares from village to village. 2: a low-class lawyer. 3: a middleman in the nail and chain trade. 4: an agricultural laborer who feeds cattle.

folio: 1: a large sheet of paper folded in half to form the pages of a book. 2: a book numbered only on one side. 3: a library designation for large oversized books.

foolscap: writing paper varying from 12 x 15 inches to 13 1/2 x 17 inches.

foot boat: a ferry boat used to carry only foot-passengers.

foot-maiden: a female attendant.

foot man: a servant who would run errands among his other duties.

foot-pad: a robber on foot.

Forbes Road: route to the West built ca. 1780 which opened passage between Philadelphia and Pittsburgh, Pennsylvania.

forbid the banns: public or formal objection to a marriage.

fore-elder: (*obsolete*) ancestor.

forestaller: one who buys goods before they come to market with the intention of raising the price.

forester: [*also* foster] an individual much like a present day game warden or forest ranger.

formulary: a book containing oaths, declarations, and prayers, written in prescribed forms.

fortnight: two weeks.

forty: one-sixteenth of a section of land, or forty acres.

fosse: a pool or moat for drowning lawbreakers.

foster: *see* forester.

foster dam: a nurse; one who takes surrogate care of a child.

founday: six days, the time iron workers needed to make eight tons of iron.

Fourteenth Colony: a settlement near Natchez, Mississippi, between 1772 and 1775, founded by the King, Swayze, Thomas, Farrar, Cory, and Horton families from New Jersey.

Fourth of July Claims: an act on 4 July 1864 making the Quartermaster General responsible for investigating and recommending settlement of "all claims of loyal citizens in states not in rebellion, for quartermaster's stores" furnished to or seized by the Union army.

Fox Indians: a tribe of Algonquin Indians along the Mississippi River.

framer: one who frames or builds the skeleton of a house; a picture framer.

frank: free; not in bondage; to enable to pass or go freely or easily.

frankalmoin: in English law, land given to a religious corporation to hold and use in exchange for praying for the soul of the donor.

franklin: a fifteenth-century English freeholder; a middle class land owner.

Franklin: the "State of Franklin" was organized in 1784 in the western part of North Carolina, and ceased to exist in 1788.

frank marriage: the tenure by which a man and his wife held an estate granted by a blood relative of the wife in consideration of their marriage. The tenure was to be held of the donor by the children of the couple to the fourth generation with no other service to the grantor than their faithfulness.

frankpledge: a medieval English system under which each male member of a tithing, twelve years of age or upwards, was responsible for the good conduct of other members.

frater: (*Lat.*) brother; cousin; brother-in-law; kinsman.

fra will: below forty pounds (sterling).

fream: ploughed land that has been worked too much and needs to lie fallow.

freedman: a male released from slavery; one who is emancipated.

freedom dues: upon completion of an indenture or apprenticeship contract, the payment of dues by the master to the apprentice or servant.

freedom right: an indentured servant's right to a specified amount of acreage at the end of his term of service.

free from restraint: a condition that must be met before a will is valid, which is that the maker of the will is free of any undue force or persuasion when he made and signed the will.

freehold: an estate held outright with no other claims on it and which may be transferred to heirs or others.

freeholder: a person who owns property rather than rents it; one in possession of a freehold.

freeman: 1: in general, a white male over 21 years of age, free to ply a trade, own land, and to vote. 2: (*American Old South*) freed slaves or anyone who was taxable or could vote.

free man of color: a black man free from the time of his birth, or who was freed later in life.

freemasons: begun in England (1st Grand Lodge, 1725) by stone cutters, it soon came to include men of means and nobility. It puts forth social reform principles and the ideals of fraternity, equality of men, and peace. In 1733, the First Lodge of Boston was established.

free papers: (*American Old South*) a document (certificate, certified registration, etc.) stamped with a court seal provided by a county, city, or town to a free black as evidence of freedom.

free socage: *see* socage.

French Grant: land donated in 1795 by Congress to a group of French people swindled by a land company, located in Scioto County, Ohio.

French Republican calendar: *see* Republican calendar.

French Spoliation Cases: cases brought before the U.S. Court of Claims from 1793 to 1801 to seek redress for American merchants who suffered the loss of ships and goods at the hands of French warships.

friar: a member of a religious order, especially one of the four mendicant monastic orders, in the Roman Catholic Church. The orders were known as the Franciscans, Augustinians, Dominicans, and Carmelites.

Friendly Society: a public business required to buy a permit or license, thus contributing to the community through indirect tax.

frigate: a fast, lightweight warship of the eighteenth and nineteenth century, which carried up to sixty guns; any small sailing vessel.

Frimaire: in the Republican Calendar, the month of frost.

fripperer: one who buys and sells old clothes.

frippery: a shop where old clothes are sold.

friseur: a hair dresser.

froe: [also frow] a wedge-shaped cleaving tool.

Fructidor: in the Republican calendar, the month of fruit.

fruiterer: a person who buys and sells fruit; a ship that transfers fruit.

fruitestere: a female fruit seller.

fulker: a pawnbroker or money lender.

full age: adult.

fuller: 1: a person who fulls cloth by increasing the weight and bulk of fabric by shrinking, beating, or pressing it. 2: a tool used by blacksmiths to hammer grooves into iron.

fulling mill: a mill where cloth is fulled by means of pestles or stampers which clean, beat, and press it to a compact state.

funambulist: a tightrope walker or dancer.

funebris: (*Lat.*) funeral; deadly; mortal.

funereus: (*Lat.*) funeral; deadly; destructive.

funero: (*Lat.*) to kill; ruin; death.

furbisher: a person who polishes armor.

furlong: a distance equal to 1/8 of a mile, which is forty rods, poles, or perches, 220 yards, 660 feet, or ten chains.

furner: a baker; one in charge of the ovens.

furniture: originally, the items necessary to equip a man and a horse; later, any kind of moveable property, including livestock.

furrier: one who buys, sells, and/or makes furs.

furuncle: a small tumor or boil, with inflammation and pain, under the skin.

fusil: 1: in heraldry, a sub-ordinary on a shield which is placed on the field and is lozenge-shaped, longer than it is wide. 2: a musket.

fusileer: a soldier armed with a fusil.

fustian: originally, a coarse cloth made of a cotton and linen; later, corduroy, velveteen, etc.

G

gabel: 1: to make a mark on a sheep's ear for identification purposes. 2: an excise tax.

gabeler: a tax or gabelle collector.

gabelle: a tax, especially the tax levied on salt in France before the Revolution of 1789.

gad: a stake, spike of metal, or sharp pointed rod.

gad bit: a nail passer.

Gadsden Purchase: the purchase of the southern Arizona area in 1853 from Mexico.

gaffer: 1: an old man, usually from the country. 2: a headman or foreman of a work gang.

gager: one who assesses and collects taxes on the contents of casks of liquor.

gainage: the horses, oxen and furniture of the wain, or the instruments for carrying on tillage; the land itself, or the profit made by cultivation.

gaiter: a spat or legging made of cloth or leather, usually strapped under the shoe; a form of high-topped shoe.

gall: a sore on the skin caused by chafing or rubbing; bile.

galloping consumption: acute active pulmonary (lung) tuberculosis.

gallows: [*also* gallusesa] man's suspenders.

galluses: suspenders.

gallusesa: *see* gallows.

galvanized yankee: a Confederate soldier who enlisted in the Union army and saw duty on the western frontier.

gammer: an old woman.

gangrel: a vagrant or roving beggar.

gangsman: a foreman; a dockporter.

gangweek: Rogation week, the time when the boundaries of the parishes were formerly surveyed.

ganneker: an alehouse keeper.

gaol: (*obsolete*) jail.

gaol delivery: an early American Superior Court of special jurisdiction.

gaoler: (*obsolete*) a jailer.

garcion: a servingman or groom, usually a young man or boy.

gardianus: (*Lat.*) church warden.

gardyloo: a cry used to warn passers-by to beware of slop thrown from a window.

garthman: 1: one who owned or worked in a fish-garthe (a dam in a river for catching fish). 2: a yardman or herdsman.

gastrocele: a ruptured stomach.

gatehouse: a lodge or house for a servant or gatekeeper near the entrance of a park or large estate.

gate-schadylle: (*obsolete*) *a* crossway in the road; a parting of the ways.

gathering: a collection of pus; an abscess.

Gatherite: *see* Cutlerite.

gavelkind: a tenure in which a father's estate was divided equally among his sons.

geld: a tax paid by the landholders to the Saxon and Norman Kings.

geldable: liable to taxes.

gemelli: (*Lat.*) [*also* gemellu; geminus] twin; twin-born.

gemmary: [*also* gemmery] any thing pertaining to gems, such as a case or house; gems collectively.

General Society of Colonial Wars: a group organized in 1893 for adult males with lineal descent from an ancestor who rendered military or civil service to the colonies from 1607 to 1775.

General Society of Mayflower Descendants: a society organized in 1897 for descendants (over 18) of passengers *Mayflower* on the voyage that terminated at Plymouth in December, 1620.

General Society of the War of 1812: [*originally* Defenders of Baltimore] a society organized in 1814 for males (over 21) who are lineal descendants of a participant during the War of 1812 in the Army, Navy, Revenue-Marine, or Privateer Service of the United States.

General Society, Sons of the Revolution: a society founded in 1876 for male lineal descendants, on either parent's side, of a military or naval veteran of the forces of the Thirteen Colonies, Continental Congress, or other bodies which remained loyal to the American cause.

genero: (*Lat.*) to beget; to bring to life.

generosa: (*Lat.*) lady.

generosus: (*Lat.*) gentleman, of noble birth; servant of good.

genetrix: (*Lat.*) mother.

genitalis: (*Lat.*) birth.

gentilis: (*Lat.*) of the same clan or race.

gentle craft: 1: fishing. 2: shoemaking.

gentlewoman: a woman of good family or breeding; a woman who has the occupation of waiting on or caring for a person of high rank.

gentry: persons of good breeding; those between the nobility and the yeomanry.

genus: (*Lat.*) origin; race; family; ancestry.

Geofile: an alphabetical gazetteer of about 65,000 place-names and geographical features for the greater Southwest including all of California, Arizona, New Mexico, Texas (below 32 degrees north latitude), and northern Mexico (above 22 degrees north latitude).

geographer's line: a line surveyed by Thomas Hutchins in accordance with the ordinance of 1785, starting where the Pennsylvania border intersected the Ohio River and ran due west, south of which were the "Seven Ranges."

geometer: a person skilled in geometry.

germana: (*Lat.*) a full sister.

germani: brother.

germanus: (*Lat.*) 1: having the same parents. 2: full brother.

Germinal: in the Republican Calendar, the month of seeds.

gerrymander: a division or arrangement of a voting district made to favor one candidate over another.

gerund grinder: a teacher who instructs Latin grammar.

gestour: a storyteller.

gift causa mortis: a gift given by someone who is approaching death.

gig: 1: a taxable item in 1860. 2: an open, two-wheeled carriage pulled by a horse. *See* timwhiskey.

gigno: (*Lat.*) to beget; to bear; to be born.

gild: a tax.

gilder: one whose occupation it is to overlay an item with gold leaf.

gill: 1: a one-fourth pint liquid measure. 2: malt liquor medicated with ground ivy.

ginour: an engineer.

girdler: one who makes girdles.

Gladdenite: *see* Cutlerite.

gladstone bag: a hinged traveling bag that could be opened flat into two equal compartments.

glazier: a glass cutter; a person who glazes pottery, paper, etc.

glebe: land belonging to a parish or benefice given to the minister to use during his ministry.

glebe terrier: a book in which the church leadership kept track of land assigned to the ministers of the churches.

glos: (*Lat.*) sister-in-law.

glove money: 1: a gratuity given to servants to buy gloves. 2: (*England*) the rewards given to officers of courts.

godcept: (*obsolete*) gossip.

godphere: a godfather

gold house: a treasury.

goldsmith: a banker; one who deals in articles made of gold; a craftsman who makes vessels and ornaments of gold.

good brother: a brother-in-law.

goodman: a man ranking below a gentleman but above a freeman.

good mother: a mother-in-law; a stepmother.

goods and chatties: personal property—goods meant inanimate objects, chatties were livestock.

good sister: a sister-in-law.

good son: a son-in-law.

goodwife: the wife or mistress of a household.

goody: a woman or housewife, especially an old woman.

goody-madam: a lady from a lower social status.

goose: an iron with a handle resembling a goose neck used by a tailor; a smoothing iron.

goose herd: one who herds geese.

goose herder: an itinerant tailor.

gore: a county subdivision in Maine and Vermont.

gospeller: one who "reads" the gospel in church services.

gossib: formerly, a sponsor at baptism; later, a gossip.

gossip: a godparent or baptismal sponsor.

gossips wheel: a spinning wheel designed to be used by two persons at once.

gouge: a chisel with a curved cutting edge.

grace wife: a midwife.

graduate: a physician.

grafter: a notary or scrivener.

grainer: 1: one who produced artificial grain in wood. 2: a tool used by a person who removed hair from animal hides.

grandaevus: (*Lat.*) of great age; old.

grandam: a grandmother or old woman.

Grand Army of the Republic: a group founded in Illinois in 1866, it became the largest organization of Union Veterans of the Civil War. Membership in the GAR naturally dwindled until there were 65,000 members in 1923 and only one remaining veteran in 1956 when the society was officially disbanded.

grandfather clause: an exception to a law, such as the right for blacks to vote, which gave only those blacks whose parents had voted before 1867 the right to vote.

grand patent: an original patent.

graner: a utensil used in a brewery or granary.

Grange: *see* Patrons of Husbandry.

grange: a farmhouse or small hamlet; a center of cultivation owned by a monastery, but too far away for the monks to work it.

granger: a farmer, bailiff, or steward of a farm.

grantee: the buyer, purchaser, or receiver of real or personal property rights from the seller or grantor, usually by a deed or through a trust document.

grantor: the seller or person who sells, grants, transfers, or conveys real or personal property or property rights to the purchaser, buyer, or receiver, usually by a deed or through a trust document.

Granville District: the northern half of North Carolina which was given to John Baron Carteret, the second Earl Granville, as a proprietary grant in 1744 and kept by his family until the Revolution. Unoccupied lands in this area were transferred by deeds from the earl to the grantee and were called "Granville Grants."

grapnel: a device with a hook or pronged ends, used for grasping or holding things such as food and milk.

grass widow: an unmarried woman with a child; a divorced or separated woman; a discarded mistress.

gravel: a deposit of small calculous concretions (stones) in the kidneys and bladder.

graver: one who carves or engraves letters or figures in stone; an engraving tool.

gravida: (*Lat.*) pregnant; with child.

grayback: [*also* gray coat; gray jacket] Confederate soldiers during the American Civil War.

Graybeard Regiment: a Union regiment, the 37th Iowa Volunteer Infantry, composed of old men, and assembled at Camp Strong, near Muscatine, Iowa.

gray coat: [*also* gray jacket] *see* grayback

grazier: one who pastures and raises cattle for market.

greatest creditor: the person to whom the most is owed by a deceased person.

Great Genesee Road: a route between Utica, New York, and Cleveland, Ohio, as a path to the West.

Great Registers: voter lists or voter registration lists, in California, Nevada, Arizona, and Hawaii.

Great Survey: any of the 37 independent surveys conducted by the U.S. government which established the base lines and prime meridians creating 37 independent survey systems.

Great Valley Road: a road leading to the South and the West starting in southeastern Pennsylvania, going through the Shenandoah Valley, Knoxville, Tennessee, and into Huntsville, Alabama.

greave: [*also* grieve] 1: a bailiff, foreman, or sheriff. 2: a boot providing an armor for the legs.

Greenbrier Company: a company founded by John Robinson, John Vanmeter, Robert Beverley, and Benjamin Bordon in 1751, which was granted 100,000 acres of land in Virginia. In exchange, they were to survey and sell all the land to settlers within a specified length of time.

green-grocer: a retailer of greens.

green sickness: anemia; chlorosis; a disease of young women giving the complexion a greenish tinge.

Gregorian calendar: named after Pope Gregory, but referred to as the "New Style" calendar which replaced the Julian calendar in 1582 in some countries. In Great Britain, her colonies (American), and other protestant countries it was not adopted until 1752.

grieve: *see* greave.

griff: [*also* griffe] a child having one black parent and the other parent a mulatto; a child of a black and an American Indian.

grimgribber: a lawyer; the legal jargon of a lawyer.

grindery: 1: materials used by a shoemaker and leathers used by other workers. 2: a place that grinds and sharpens knives, blades, saws, etc.

griot: an African clan's story teller or oral historian.

grippe: influenza.

groat: a small sum; an old English coin worth four pence.

grocer's itch: a cutaneous disease caused by mites in sugar and flour.

grog: a mixture of rum and water named after Old Grog, the nickname given to Admiral Vernon, who introduced the drink about 1745.

groggery: a tavern.

groom grubber: an officer in the English Royal Household.

groom porter: an officer of the English Royal Household whose principal functions were to regulate all matters connected with gaming within the courts, to furnish cards and dice, and to decide disputes.

groove: a mine shaft or pit.

groover: a miner.

ground rent: rent paid on land.

guardian: a person appointed by the court to take care of someone unable to care for himself, such as a minor, an incompetent, an invalid, an idiot, etc.

guardian ad litem: a guardian appointed by the court to take care of a special matter before the court, such as a lawsuit.

guardian bond: bond posted by a guardian to insure his/her carrying out the responsibilities in the manner required by the court.

Guardians of the Poor: unions formed in 1834 in England to take over care of the poor from the parishes.

guild: a medieval association of merchants and craftsmen which regulated price, quality, and decided who could make and sell the merchandise under its supervision.

guilder: a gold or silver coin in the Netherlands, Germany, and Austria.

gules: in heraldry, the color red represented by vertical hatching (lines drawn vertically) in black and white drawings.

gundalow: cargo carrying river sail boats.

Gunter's chain: a unit of measurement (sixty-six feet) used by a surveyor.

Gunter's scale: a scale with natural and logarithmic lines and used in solving problems in navigation and surveying.

gutter-blood: a base born or low bred person.

guttersnipe: 1: a slum child. 2: a small handbill used for advertising.

H

habendum et tenendum: (*Lat.*) *literally* "to have and to hold to the grantee (buyer or donee) his heirs and assigns"; a clause in a deed that specifies the type of property or estate that the buyer will receive.

haberdasher: a person who sells men's furnishings, such as hats, shirts, neckties, handkerchiefs, gloves, etc.

habitacle: a dwelling; an alcove.

hac: (*Lat.*) byway; this way; this side; here; hither.

hacker: one who makes or uses hoes, mattocks, etc.

hackle: a device that separates the coarse part of flax or hemp from the fine.

hackney: a hired carriage or horse; a hired menial worker.

hackney man: one who rents horses and carriages.

haemoptysis: *see* hemoptysis.

haggler: a huckster.

half-baptized: baptized at home instead of church.

half blood: the condition of being a half brother or sister—half brothers and sisters are known as brothers and sisters by the half blood, because they only have one common parent, while those from the same parents are said to be of the whole blood. If no provision is made each child inherits from the natural parent and takes nothing from the step parent.

half-haque: [*also* half-hagg] *see* demihag.

half orphan: a child who had lost only one parent—used by the New York Children's Aid Society.

half pay pension: half the usual or full wages given to an officer in the army or navy when retired or not in actual service.

halfpenny: a British bronze coin, dating from Anglo-Saxon times, of the value of half a penny, or two farthings.

hallage: a fee paid for goods sold in a hall.

Hamburg Passenger lists: lists which include emigrants

from Austria, Hungary, Poland, Russia, Czechoslovakia, and of course Germany for the period from 1850 to 1934 (1915-19 missing due to World War I).

hand woman: a midwife; a female attendant.

hangby: a dependent.

hank: a measurement of cotton or woolen yarn, cotton measuring 840 yards and wool 560 yards per hank.

harbinger: in England, an officer of the king who rode a day's journey ahead of the court to find accommodations.

hard-shell: 1: rigid and uncompromising in religious orthodoxy. 2: a member of the more conservative of the two factions of the Democratic party in New York state in 1852 and following years.

Hardshell Baptists: a strict sect of Baptists with extreme Calvinistic views.

hardy: [*also* hardie] a chisel-like tool with a square shank set into a hole in an anvil, used for cutting off pieces from iron rods.

harmer-beck: a constable.

harper: an old Irish coin with the image of a harp on one side.

hasp: a measurement of linen or woolen yam which is a fourth part of a spindle (14,400 yards in linen or 15,120 yards in cotton).

hasty pudding: mush made of oatmeal or flour.

hatchel: an instrument for combing flax or hemp.

hatcheler: one who cleans or dresses flax.

hauling regulars: men who hauled goods on a regular basis.

hawker: an itinerant peddler or huckster. *See* badger.

hayward: an official in charge of public fencing and impounding stray animals.

head money: 1: a poll tax. 2: a bounty per head for captured prisoners.

headright certificate: a document obtained by a person qualifying for a headright grant.

headright claim: a claim to land based on the headright system of granting land to induce settlement in American Colonies.

headright grant: a land grant system introduced to attract people to the colonies, under which each head of family who emigrated to the colonies was given fifty acres of land providing he settled on it and improved the land and paid a fee to the Crown.

headsman: 1: an executioner. 2: in a colliery, one who removes the coal from the workings to the tramway.

headswoman: a midwife.

hearth money: a tax assessed for each fireplace in the home, usually two shillings per hearth.

hearth tax: begun in 1660 in England, a tax based on the number of fireplaces in a home, unless exempted by poverty.

heat sickness: a condition marked especially by cessation of sweating and extremely high body temperature, caused by a loss of salt from the body.

hectare: a metric measure equal to 10,000 square meters.

hectical complaint: 1: in medicine, a remittent fever with stages of chilliness, heat, and sweat. 2: (*rare*) a person suffering with tuberculosis.

hedge-priest: an illiterate or uneducated priest.

hedger: one who plants or trims hedges.

hedge school: an Irish school held in the open air, hence a poor, low-class school.

heel cutter: a tool used for cutting out lifts for the heel of a boot or shoe.

heer: a measurement of linen or woolen yarn which contains two cuts, the sixth part of a hasp or hank of yarn.

heir apparent: a person who is the rightful heir and most likely to receive the estate if he survives the ancestor.

heir-at-law: the person (commonly the eldest son) to whom all of an intestate's real property was due under the system of primogeniture.

heirs and assigns: insuring that absolute ownership was given—used in deeds, wills, conveyances, and considered essential in these documents.

heling: a bed coverlet.

hellier: a tiler or slater.

helmet: in heraldry, the part of a coat of arms which bears the crest.

hematemesis: vomiting blood.

hematuria: a discharge of bloody urine.

hemiplegy: a palsy or paralysis that affects one side of the body.

hemoptysis: [*also* haemoptysis] spitting up blood from the larynx, trachea, bronchi, or lungs.

hempheckler: a flax dresser.

henter: a thief.

hera: (*Lat.*) mistress of a house; lady.

herald: an officer in Great Britain whose duty is to take charge of public ceremonies and to record and blazon the arms of the upper class and to regulate any abuses which may occur.

heraldry: the art or office of a herald; the art, practice, or science of recording genealogies and blazoning arms or ensigns armorial.

heredis: (*Lat.*) heir.

hereditament: anything that can be inherited, whether real or personal property—tangible property is considered corporeal hereditament and anything intangible, such as an easement or rent, is considered incorporeal hereditament.

Hereditary Order of Descendants of the Loyalists and Patriots of the American Revolution: a group organized in 1973 for adults descended from both a loyalist and a patriot of the American Revolution.

Hereditary Order of the Descendants of Colonial Governors: a group founded in 1896 for adults who have a proven descent from one or more of the accepted colonial governors.

hereditas: (*Lat.*) heirship; inheritance.

heriot: a fine paid by a villein, or sometimes a freeholder, to his lord when he inherited copyhold land; estate duty.

herpes zoster: *see* shingles.

herus: (*Lat.*) master of the house or family; lord.

Hessian: German protestants native to the Hesse, Germany area who settled originally in South Carolina; German troops sent to help King George III put down his rebellious colonies.

heusire: a payment to an overlord by the tenant for the right to hold a manorial court.

hewing dog: a piece of iron made to hold a small log in place while it was shaped with an axe.

hic: (*Lat.*) here; in this manner.

hic jacet: (*Lat.*) here lies.

hic jacet sepultus: (*Lat.*) here lies buried.

hic requiescit in pace: (*Lat.*) [*abbrev.* h.r.i.p.] here rests in peace.

hic situs: (*Lat.*) [*abbrev.* h.s.] here is buried.

hide of land: a land measurement which varied from 80 to 120 acres; a common measurement in the Domesday Book, it represented an amount of land that would support a family, or as much land as one could plow in a year's time.

higger: a person who peddles merchandise.

higgler: an itinerant dealer who carries his wares on his back.

High Court of Admiralty: *see* admiralty court.

High Court of Chancery: in England, the highest court of justice next to Parliament.

highwayman: a robber who works the public roads.

high yellow: a light colored black or a mulatto of superior birth or manners.

hind: farm laborer, household or domestic servant.

hip gout: osteomyelitis.

hired man: a gardener; stableman; farmhand.

Historical Records Survey: (1936-43) during the post war period, a Works Progress Administration inventory of records in public facilities throughout the country.

hobbler: 1: a soldier on horse-back. 2: one who tows a boat with a rope along a river bank.

hobby: a medium sized, vigorous horse.

hobbyhorse: one of the early forms of bicycles propelled by pushing with the feet on the ground.

Hocktide: the second Monday and Tuesday after Easter.

hoc loco: (*Lat.*) in this place.

hoc mense: (*Lat.*) in this month.

hoc tempore: (*Lat.*) at this time.

hodman: a mason's helper; a tray used for carrying mortar and bricks carried on the shoulder.

hogshead: a cask with the capacity of 60 to 140 gallons of liquid or 750 to 1,200 pounds of tobacco.

hoir: (*obsolete*) heir.

Holland Society of New York: a society founded in 1885 for male descendants of settlers in the Dutch colonies in North America prior to 1675.

holograph: a document prepared completely in the handwriting of the person making the document, and signed with their signature.

holographic will: [*also* olographic] a will written entirely by hand and bearing the date and having the signature of the testator.

Holy Thursday: the Thursday before Easter.

Holy Week: the week before Easter, in which the passion of Christ is commemorated.

homage: in feudal law, the submission, loyalty, and service a tenant promised to his lord when first admitted to the land which he held of him in fee; the act of the tenant in making this submission, on being invested with the fee.

Home for Little Wanderers, The New England: an organization founded in Boston in 1865 to place orphaned children. *See* Children's Aid Society.

home lot: the plot of ground where the home was built on a large farm including the area around the house enclosed by a high fence on which a garden was grown and animals kept.

homespun: cloth spun at home.

homestead: the house and adjoining land where the head of the family lives, which passes to the widow when her husband dies and is exempt from the claims of his creditors—this is similar to a widow's dower, the difference being that the homestead includes the dwelling. Minor children are also entitled to homestead if both parents are deceased. A wife may forfeit her right to the homestead if she is guilty of misconduct or abandonment.

Homestead Act: any of several legislative acts authorizing the sale of public land.

homestead lands: public lands disposed of through the homestead process.

honour: a large estate with several manor houses ruled over by one lord.

hoofer: a professional dancer.

hookah: [also hooka] a smoking pipe with a long flexible stem that cools smoke by passing it through water.

hoop: a measure of capacity used in England.

hooper: a cooper; one who puts the hoops on casks or tubs.

hoosier: a native of Indiana.

hora: (Lat.) hour; season (of the year).

hornbook: 1: an elementary treatise. 2: a piece of wood with pieces of translucent horn attached to both sides containing a piece of paper marked with the alphabet.

horrors: delirium tremens.

horse coper: a horse dealer or breeder.

horse courser: a man who keeps race horses.

horse knave: a groom.

horse leech: 1: a veterinarian. 2: a farrier or beggar.

horseways: a cart road; a road on which a horse can pass.

hostel: an inn or place of lodging.

hosteler: one who receives and lodges guests; a student who lives in a hostel.

hostilement: a household item such as furniture, a utensil, or an implement.

hostler: 1: a stableman or groom. 2: one who services railroad engines.

hot house: a bathhouse.

houseage: a fee for keeping goods.

house joiner: one who builds house frames.

housel: (*obsolete*) the Holy Eucharist.

housewife: [*also* hussy] a small sewing case used in the military.

housewright: a house builder.

howdy wife: a midwife.

huckster: a peddler or salesman. *See* badger.

huggah: (*Arabic*) a round box or a bottle through which tobacco fumes pass.

Huguenot: French Protestant who migrated to America in 1721.

Huguenot Society of America: a group founded in 1883 for adult lineal descendants of Huguenot families who immigrated to America prior to the Edict of Toleration, 28 November 1787.

hujus mense: (*Lat.*) this month's.

humanitian: a grammarian.

hundred: 1: county subdivision in Delaware. 2: originally, enough land to support one hundred families.

Huntington's chorea: a nervous disorder, accompanied by increasing mental deterioration.

hurdling bill: a tool used to make wattle hurdles.

Huron: [*also* Wyandot] Indian native to Canada and the northeastern United States.

husbandman: a farmer; a master of a family.

husking pin: a peg or pin attached to the hand to help remove husks from corn.

hussar: 1: a robber. 2: a light-armed cavalryman.

Hussite: (*slang*) a religious reform zealot.

hussy: 1: a small sewing kit, often carried by men in the military. *See* housewife. 2: a housewife or thrifty woman.

Hutterites: a religious group founded by Jacob Hutter (Austrian reformer) in 1500s, part of the Anabaptist movement.

hydrocephalus: [*also* dropsy of the brain] an abnormal increase in the amount of fluid in the cranium, causing enlargement of the head and loss of mental powers.

hydropericardium: heart dropsy.

hydrophobia: 1: a preternatural dread of water. 2: a symptom of canine madness (rabies).

hydrops: dropsy.

hydrothorax: dropsy in the chest; an abnormal amount of fluid in the pleural cavity.

hyertropy of heart: enlargement of the heart.

hypothecation: the pledging of property, such as land or a ship, to secure a loan. *See* bottomry.

hysterotomy: in surgery, a Cesarean section.

I

iacet hic: (*Lat.*) here lies.

iceman: an ice dealer; one who delivers ice to customers.

icterus: jaundice.

idem: (*Lat.*) the same

idem quod: (*Lat.*) the same as.

idem sonans: (*Lat.*) sounding the same.

idlemen: 1: a gentleman. 2: one with no occupation.

ignoramus: originally, the word written by a grand jury on an indictment thrown out for lack of evidence.

ignotus: (*Lat.*) unknown; low born.

ileus: an obstruction of the intestines resulting in severe constipation and pain.

ille: (*Lat.*) he; she; it; that one; the aforesaid; the very same.

immersion: baptism by complete submersion in water.

imparle: a delay in a court case in the hope of a settlement out of court.

impetigo: [*also* scrumpox] any of certain contagious skin diseases characterized by the eruption of pustules, caused by staphylococci.

importation: the act of bringing goods, merchandise, or other persons into one country from another country.

impressed seamen: seamen impressed (forced) into service on foreign ships.

imprimis: (*Lat.*) in the first place; chiefly; especially.

imprint: a note on the title page or at the end of a book, giving the publisher's name and the time and place of publication.

impropriate: an ecclesiastical benefice annexed to a corporation or lay person as their personal property, with the care of the property given to a vicar.

incognitus: (*Lat.*) unknown.

incola: (*Lat.*) [*also* incolant] an inhabitant.

incommode: to inconvenience or cause distress.

incompertus: (*Lat.*) unknown.

incorporeal property: without physical existence, but belonging as a right to a material thing or property such as a copyright.

inde: (*Lat.*) thence; from that place; from that time.

indefeasible: interest or ownership in property, or an estate in fee simple, which cannot be voided, taken away, or defeated—indefeasible rights to property can be inherited.

indented servant: *see* indentured servant.

indenture: 1: an agreement or deed between two or more parties conveying real estate, originally made in two parts so that it could be separated by tearing in a jagged line and matched later. 2: a contract in which a person is bound over for service.

indentured servant: [*also* bond servant] a servant who sold himself to a master for a period of time (usually 4 to 7 years) in order to pay for passage to another country. The contract was transferrable, saleable, and was passed on to heirs if the master died

independent city: a city which no longer falls under the jurisdiction of the county in which it lies.

Independents: *see* Separatists.

indictment: a document based on a decision by a grand jury that sufficient evidence exists to bring a person to trial.

indidem: (*Lat.*) from the same place or thing.

indigent: a pauper.

indirect tax: tax from sources other than property or income, such as businesses, professions, entertainment, and animals.

indiscriminate survey: a survey not tied to any large survey grid, strictly speaking—often incorrectly referred to as metes and bounds because it incorporated the use of compass bearings.

ineditus: (*Lat.*) not published; not made known.

in esse: (*Lat.*) in being; in existence.

in extremis: (*Lat.*) in the final stage of life; in his last moments.

infamy: loss of character and certain civil rights by a person convicted of an infamous crime.

infans: (*Lat.*) childish; little child.

infans cui quis in baptismo sponsor exstitit: (*Lat.*) godchild.

infantile paralysis: *see* poliomylitis.

infirmarian: a person who works in or has charge of an infirmary.

in forma pauperis: (*Lat.*) *literally* "in the manner of a pauper"; a court procedure allowing a pauper to file a lawsuit, even though the pauper does not have enough money to pay court costs.

infra: (*Lat.*) below; beneath.

in genere: (*Lat.*) in the same quality and quantity; in kind.

in loco: (*Lat.*) in the place.

in loco citata: (*Lat.*) in the place cited.

in loco parentis: (*Lat.*) in the place of parents.

inlot: a lot surveyed and platted within a new or established town or village.

inmate: 1: a prisoner. 2: a border or renter of land whose personal property is taxable or who was treated as faculty. *See* faculty.

innholder: an innkeeper.

in nomine Domini: (*Lat.*) in the name of the Lord.

innubus: (*Lat.*) unmarried.

innupta: (*Lat.*) unmarried.

in perpetuam: (*Lat.*) forever.

in personam: (*Lat.*) over persons.

in posse: (*Lat.*) potentially; possibly.

inquilinus: (*Lat.*) of foreign birth; a lodger.

inquisition: an investigation, in law; in inquest.

inquisitions post damnum: (*Lat.*) inquiries made regarding loss of revenue caused by a tenant's actions.

inquisitions post mortem: (*Lat.*) inquiries made on the death of an estate owner regarding the amount due prior to inheritance.

in rem: (*Lat.*) over things.

in room of: in the place of.

insolvent estate: one in which the widow receives one third and the creditors the remainder.

in specie: (*Lat.*) specific; identifiable.

instant: the same as is given.

in stirpes: (*Lat.*) *see* per stirpes.

institus: (*Lat.*) inborn; natural adopted.

intelligencer: 1: a spy. 2: a newsletter or newspaper.

intendant: one who is in charge of or directs a public business.

intentions: *see* banns.

intermarriage: the condition of a marriage contract being a reciprocal and mutual engagement by which each of the parties was married to the other—this has nothing to do with the parties being related to each other.

inter: (*Lat.*) between; among; in comparison.

inter alia: (*Lat.*) among other things.

interfactor: a murderer.

interrogatory: questions asked and statements taken from absentee witnesses to be included in depositions during court trials.

in terrorem clause: a provision in a will that warns heirs of limitations which could result in disinheritance.

intervention: in law, the act where a third party interposes and becomes a party to an ongoing suit pending between two other persons.

inter vivos: (*Lat.*) between the living.

intestacy: to die without leaving a valid will.

intestinal colic: pain throughout the abdomen, usually caused by an improper diet.

in toto: (*Lat.*) in the whole; entirely.

intra quattuor maria: (*Lat.*) within the four seas.

intussusception: the condition where part of the intestine has slipped into another part just below it.

inuptus: (*Lat.*) [*also* inupta] unmarried.

in ventre sa mere: (*Lat.*) *literally* "in his mother's womb"; a child who has been conceived but has not yet been born.

in vita testatorius: (*Lat.*) in the testator's lifetime.

ipse fecit: (*Lat.*) he did it himself.

ipso facto: (*Lat.*) by the act itself.

ironmaster: the owner or manager of an iron foundry.

Iroquois Trail: a colonial highway between the Hudson and Niagara rivers.

Irvingite: in England, an adherent of the Catholic Apostolic Church after a preacher, Edward Irving.

ischewe: (*obsolete*) issue or progeny.

issue: lineal descendants of a common ancestor.

item: a term marking the beginning of a paragraph in a will.

itinerant occupation: an occupation practiced by a person who traveled around the country offering their services, such as dancing masters, lecturers, preachers, mimics, school teachers, magic shows, singing groups, etc.

J

jack: 1: a male donkey (a taxable item in 1860). 2: a common fellow, boy assistant, sailor, or lumberjack.

Jackson Purchase: an area in Tennessee, known as "Grants West of the Tennessee River," acquired by U.S. in 1818 including the counties of McCracken, Ballard, Carlisle, Hickman, Fulton, Graves, Marshall, and Calloway.

jade: a worthless horse.

jagger: a carrier, carter, peddler or hawker; in mining, a man who carries ore on a pack-horse from a mine to the smelter; a boy who has charge of the jags or train or trucks in a coal mine.

jail fever: typhus.

jalap: a purgative medicine made from the root of the Mexican jalap.

Jamestown Society: a society founded in 1936 for descendants of stockholders in the Virginia Company of London, settlers at Jamestown or on Jamestown Island before 1700.

jarvey: a hackney coach, or the person who drives one.

jaundice: a condition caused by obstruction of bile and characterized by yellowness of the skin, fluids, and tissues, and by constipation, loss of appetite, and weakness.

javel: a vagabond.

jerico: a place where a person would go if he/she wished retirement or concealment.

Jim-crow: a black man—used in a hostile way.

jobber: 1: a person who buys in quantity and sells to individual dealers. 2: one who works by the job or does piecework. 3: a person who works in an official capacity and is dishonest, using the office for his own gain.

joe: a four-penney piece.

Johnnie: [*also* Johnny] a Confederate soldier in the American Civil War.

johnny-cake: a cake or bread consisting of cornmeal or wheatmeal, toasted on a griddle.

joiner: a carpenter who does interior finish work.

joint tenancy: the condition of two or more persons owning a piece of property—this type of ownership allows all persons to use the property and share in it equally.

jointure: an estate secured for the wife instead of a dower, only to be used by the wife until death.

joint will: [*also* conjoint will] a will signed by two or more persons, allowing a couple's separately held land to be treated as a common fund.

jongleur: an itinerant minstrel.

jottour: [*also* jorre] juror, jury.

jouster: hawker or peddler of fish.

Jr.: *see* Junior.

juba: 1: crest of a helmet in a coat of arms. 2: a dance with a lively rhythm and hand clapping performed by Southern blacks.

Jubiliati: a moveable feast day.

jure uxoris: the third Sunday after Easter.

Judica: a moveable feast day, the fifth Sunday in Lent, the second before Easter.

jugo: (*Lat.*) to marry; to join.

Julian calendar: a calendar named for Julius Caesar, it is referred to as the "Old Style" calendar, which was used from 45 BC until 1582, when it was replaced by the Gregorian calendar.

jumper: 1: one who delivers packages or messages from a delivery truck. 2: a religious sect of Calvinists so named because of their violent agitations and motions during worship.

Junior: [*also* Jr.] the younger of two persons having the same name—the two persons were not necessarily related, especially before the nineteenth century. When the older of the two died the younger often assumed the Sr. title or dropped the title altogether.

jurat: (*Lat.*) certification that a document was written by the person who signed it.

jure uxoris: (*Lat.*) in right of his wife.

jus accrescendi: (*Lat.*) right of survivorship.

justicer: one who administers justice.

juvenalis: (*Lat.*) youthful.

juvenca: (*Lat.*) 1: young cow. 2: girl.

juvenilis: (*Lat.*) youthful.

juvenis: (*Lat.*) young.: (*Lat.*) 1: young bullock. 2: young man.

K

kalender: (*obsolete*) calendar.

Kaskaskia: a French fort and Jesuit mission located on Kaskaskia Island in the Mississippi River, which was taken over by George Rogers Clark in 1778 and was the capital of the Illinois Territory from 1809 to 1818.

kedger: a fisherman, or one who peddles fish.

keeler: a shallow tub; a keelman.

keelhaul: a method of punishment in which a person is hauled under the keel of a boat, through the water, from one side to the other.

keep: the innermost and strongest part of a castle; the central tower of a medieval castle.

keeper of weights and measures: local (county) court appointed official.

keeping room: a common room used by the family and where they spend the most time.

Kentucky boat: a small flatboat designed especially for use on the small rivers in Kentucky.

ketch: a vessel with two masts, a main and mizzen-mast, usually from 100 to 250 tons burden.

keuchhusten: *see* whooping cough.

kidnapped: originally, to steal or carry off children or others in order to provide servants or laborers for the American plantations.

kimnel: a large tub for general household use such as brewing, kneading, and salting meat.

kine: (*obsolete*) cattle.

King's Evil: scrofula; it was thought that a king's touch could cure the disease, thus its name.

kiss-verse: *see* tissue ballot.

kith: one's friends, acquaintances and kinsfolk, now usually, just kinsfolk—as in kith and kin.

Kittaning Path: an Indian highway which stretched between Philadelphia, Pennsylvania, and the Allegheny Valley, passing through the Juniata Valley and the Kittaning Gorge, westward to the Allegheny and Ohio rivers.

knacker: 1: one who makes harnesses. 2: one who buys old horses and sells the flesh for dog meat, etc. 3: one who buys and wrecks old houses and sells the various parts.

knave: 1: a male child or serving boy. 2: one born in humble circumstances.

knobstickwedding: a wedding, under pressure of the parish vestry, of a pregnant woman to the father-to-be.

knockknobbier: the person whose duty it was to chase dogs out of church if they became a nuisance.

krass: an eastern European beer of low alcohol content.

kyack: a pack or pannier for horses.

L

Labadist: a follower of Jean de Labadie in the seventeenth century who believed that God deceives men, that the observance of the Sabbath is not important, and other peculiar or heretical opinions.

labor: land measure equal to 177 acres.

laborer: a man who owns no real estate and works for wages.

lacewoman: a lady's maid.

Ladies of the Grand Army of the Republic: a group organized in 1885 in combination with the laity: laymen; the people as opposed to the clergy.

ladle adz: a wood carving toot

Lady Day: see Annunciation.

lagniappes: a gift added to a purchase of a customer as a favor by the tradesman.

lance knight: a mercenary foot soldier.

lancet: a small two-edged surgical instrument.

land agent: a person responsible for talking to land purchasers, selecting and submitting an application for submission.

landau: a four-wheeled covered carriage with seats facing each other and a top with two sections which could be lowered independently.

land grabber: [also land jumper] one who takes possession of land illegally; (Ireland) one who took over a farm when a tenant was evicted.

Land Grant Act: (Morrill Act) an act of 1862 which granted public land to the states to use for the establishment of agricultural colleges.

land grave: 1: in South Carolina, one who owned 48,000 acres of land. 2: in Germany, a court with jurisdiction of a specific territory or a title for certain German princes.

Land Marker: 1: a member of the American Baptist Association. 2: a stone, tree, stake, cement casting, etc., used to mark a spot from which land measurements are made.

lands jobber: one who buys land on speculation and sells it to others.

land jumper: *see* land grabber.

landsman: an inexperienced sailor.

land waiter: a customs official who examined, weighed, and took account of goods that had just been landed (off a ship).

laniua: (*Lat.*) butcher.

lapse: the failure of a gift left in a will to take effect because of the death of the person named or some other technicality.

lapsed land: land set aside to be claimed as bounty, or land paid for but never claimed.

lapstone: a stone, held on the knees, used by a shoemaker to beat leather.

laryngismus stridulus: a condition, usually associated with boys under the age of two afflicted with rickets, in which the muscles of the voice box go into spasms causing shortness of breath and a "crowing" sound.

last: 1: a ship's cargo. 2: a measurement, usually 4,000 pounds, but varying according to the kind of article measured. 3: a mold of the human foot made of wood and used by shoemakers to shape their shoes.

lastage: a toll paid by traders attending markets and fairs where they showed their goods; a payment made to the authorities for the privilege of loading a ship; a duty levied at a port.

laster: one who works or shapes shoes on a last; a shoemaker.

Lataere: a moveable feast day, the fourth Sunday in Lent, the third before Easter.

latent: hidden or concealed.

latimer: (*Lat.*) an interpreter.

lattener: a maker of or worker in latten, a mixed metal of yellow color, either identical with or closely resembling brass.

laudanum: any of various pain killing preparations in which opium was the main ingredient.

launder: a person who washes linen.

lavender: a washerwoman.

law of entail: a law which forbids the division of large estates.

lay: 1: an ordinary person not belonging to a profession or clergy. 2: the act of imposing a tax or assessment.

lay preacher: one performing a minister's duties without being a member of the clergy.

lazar: a poor diseased person; a leper.

lazaretto: a hospital, building, or a ship where diseased persons are quarantined.

leaf hammer: a tool used by a blacksmith for making decorative wrought iron.

league: an English land measure of approximately three miles, a square league equaled 4,400 acres; an ocean measure of three nautical miles.

lease and release: a method of buying land to avoid paying English court fees, in which the land was leased for a period until all rights were finally purchased through a release.

leche: 1: a physician. 2: (obsolete) leech.

ledger: books containing costs, notes, income, etc. of a business or personal nature.

ledger stone: a large, flat, horizontal stone which covers a grave.

leech: a physician; a leech used for drawing blood.

leech-house: a hospital.

leet: (Great Britain) a court—the court-leet, or view of frankpledge, is a court of record held once a year within a particular hundred, lordship, or manor.

legacy: similar to a bequest, although it often has the meaning of money, whereas bequest usually means personal property.

legate: a cardinal or bishop sent as a papal ambassador to a sovereign power.

legatee: the person to whom a gift is given or left to in a will; any person receiving real or personal property by will.

legator: a person who makes a will and leaves property to others.

legerdemainist: a magician.

leige: (*obsolete*) liege, a lord.

leightonward: a gardener.

lend: (*obsolete*) to bequeath a life estate—found in many old wills, such wording as, '1 lend to my wife my plantation for her life," would mean that the wife would have a life estate in the plantation or have the use of it for her lifetime.

lent-evil: the ague.

leprous swine: undesirable meat, the sale of which was prohibited.

lerare: a learner; a teacher.

lessee: the person leasing the property.

lessor: the owner of property that is leased to another.

letters cum testamento annexo: (*Lat.*) *literally* "letters of administration with the will attached"; the situation where no executor was named in a will or the executor has refused to serve.

letters of reprisal: [*also* letters of marque] the written authorization for a privately owned vessel to take prizes (seize enemy vessels at sea).

letters patent: title to land. *See* patent.

letters testamentary: a document from the court allowing the executor named in the will to carry out his duties. He has no authority until this document is issued.

lever scale: *see* steelyard.

levitical degree: a degree of kinship within which a person is prohibited to marry.

lewis: an iron tool used for leverage when lifting large stones.

liber: (*Lat.*) a book of public records.

liberi: (*Lat.*) children; grandchildren.

liberty: an English division of a parish or town.

liberum animum testandi: (*Lat.*) free will in bequeathing.

libra: pound; English monetary unit.

libra status animarum: Book of the State of Souls, prepared by Catholic clergy about every 5 years.

liege: a lord to whom allegiance and service are due; a vassal bound to feudal service and allegiance.

liegeman: a vassal sworn to give service and support to his lord, who in return was required to give him protection.

lieger: a resident ambassador; (*obsolete*) ledger.

lien: a claim held by a person upon the property of another until a debt has been paid; a form of security for unpaid debts.

lientery: a flux of the bowels in which the ailments are discharged undigested.

life estate: an interest in property that lasts as long as a person lives.

liferent: property which the owner can hold for a lifetime but cannot be passed on.

lightage: a toll paid by a ship entering a port where there is a lighthouse.

lighter: a large, flat-bottomed barge used to unload and load ships where the water is too shallow for the ships to dock.

lighterman: one who owns or is employed on a lighter.

limner: one who illuminated books or parchments; one who paints or draws.

lineal: being in a direct line of descent, either male or female.

lineal consanguinity: being descended in a direct line from another such as son, father, and grandfather.

linener: a linen draper; shirtmaker.

link: a unit of measurement equaling 7.92 inches, which is 1/100th of a chain, used in measuring land.

linsey-woolsey: originally, a textile made of wool and flax, now a coarse wool woven on a cotton warp.

liquor tax: a tax levied on distilled goods by Congress.

lis pendens: notices of suits pending litigation, sometimes called equity notices; these usually involve actions concerning real property such as mortgage foreclosures.

list: official description of property assessed for the purpose of taxation.

lister: one who kept a list of persons being taxed and their property.

literator: an inferior schoolmaster; a literary man.

litigant: a person who is involved in a lawsuit.

litster: a dyer; one who dyes fabrics.

livery: the legal delivery of property into the hands of the new owner.

livery of seisin: when a copyholder (one holding land in copyhold, which was the holding of land by right of being recorded) was giving up his tenancy he would deliver a rod or staff to the lord who would pass it along to a new tenant in view of witnesses. Freeholders made the delivery with a piece of turf, a clod, or the ring from the door and handed it directly to the new owner.

livresterrieus: land books found in courthouses of French occupied areas, such as Missouri.

loadsman: a pilot of a ship or boat.

loblolly boy: a ship's doctor assistant.

lock keeper: one who oversees the locks of a canal.

loco: (*Lat.*) to place; to let for hire.

loco citato: (*Lat.*) in the place cited.

loco parentis: (*Lat.*) in the place of the parent.

locus: (*Lat.*) place; position; rank.

locus sigilli: (*Lat.*) [*abbrev.* L.S.] *literally* "the place of the seal"; the place where the seal is affixed on written documents.

lodesman: a ship's pilot or steersman.

lodged: in heraldry, a charge, such as a buck, hart, hind, etc., at rest and lying on the ground.

lombard: a banker, named after the money lenders of Lombardy; a pawnshop.

longeavus: (*Lat.*) of great age, ancient.

longest liver: the last person of the participants in a "lease for lives."

longshoreman: one who works on the waterfront loading and unloading ships.

long sickness: tuberculosis.

loresman: a teacher.

lorimer: a maker of bits and metal mounting for horse bridles, generally a maker of small ironware and a worker in wrought iron.

lot layer: one whose duty it is to oversee the laying of lots in a township.

Louisiana Colonials: a hereditary society established in 1917 for all lineal descendants from colonists in Louisiana before statehood, 30 April 1803.

love apple: a tomato, formerly thought to be poisonous.

Loyalist: one who actively supported the British during the American Revolution.

Loyal Land Company of Virginia: a company founded by a group (John Lewis, Thomas Walker, and others) organized in 1749, that received grants of land (800,000 acres) in excess of the amounts provided for under a 1705 law. In exchange for the grant, they were to survey and sell their land to individuals within a specified length of time.

ludimagister: (*Lat.*) schoolmaster.

lues venera: (*Lat.*) venereal disease.

lumbago: a pain in the loins and small of the back, such as precedes certain fevers.

lung fever: pneumonia.

lungs: a servant whose duty was to blow the fire of an alchemist.

lutestring: [*also* lustring] a soft plain silk material.

lyceum: a concert or lecture hall; an organization that provides lectures and concerts.

M

madrina: female sponsor.

madstone: [*also* snakestone] a small porous stone which supposedly absorbed venom from a snake bite and cured hydrophobia (rabies).

maiden: 1: a young unmarried woman. 2: a Scottish guillotine used for beheading criminals.

mainor: (*obsolete*) caught in the act of theft with the goods on the person, such as venison or wood.

mainpernor: in law, a surety for a prisoner's appearance in court on a specific day, different from bail, in that when a man is out on bail he may be imprisoned before the stipulated day of appearance.

mains: the lands attached to a home or farmhouse.

major: (*Lat.*) mayor.

maire: (*obsolete*) to marry.

maison: (*obsolete*) house.

maister: a master.

maisterman: a ruler; a husband.

major: a person who has reached majority (full legal age).

majores: (*Lat.*) ancestors.

majoris: (*Lat.*) greater; older.

majority: the age at which one is legally no longer a minor.

major natu: (*Lat.*) in date, prior.

mala fide: (*Lat.*) acting in bad faith.

malpresentment: unnatural presentation of a child at birth involving struggle and death.

maltster: one who makes or deals in malt.

manciple: a steward in an English college or monastery.

mango: 1: seven-eighths black. 2: a slave dealer.

mania puerperium: a mental disorder affecting new mothers.

manse: a parsonage; acreage large enough to support a family.

mantuamaker: a dressmaker.

marasmus: a disease characterized by progressive deterioration of body tissue, usually due to severe malnutrition or protracted intestinal disorders.

march: a boundary or landmark, especially applied to political boundaries.

marchale: a marshall.

Marchpane: [*also* March Pan; New Year bread] small, sweet New Year's cakes made into fancy shapes by molds.

march stone: a stone used to mark the boundary of an estate.

mariages: marriable.

marita: (*Lat.*) married woman; wife.

maritagium: (*Lat.*) marriage.

maritus: (*Lat.*) bridegroom; married man.

Marquis: a title of honor ranking below a duke and above an earl or count.

marrano: a Jew or Moor converted to Christianity to avoid persecution.

marriage by contract: a marriage under which certain conditions are stipulated in a contract regarding the disposition of land brought to the marriage by the wife or the use of a title due to social status.

marriage by dispensation: marriage in the Catholic church by virtue of exemption for a church procedure.

marriage by priest: in Society of Friends (Quaker) records, indicates the marriage of a member by a minister of another denomination.

marriage out: [*also* marriage out of unity; marriage out of meeting] the marriage of a person belonging to the Quaker faith who marries out of the church or contrary to the beliefs.

martello tower: a circular coastal fort made of stone or brick to guard against invaders.

mason: a stonecutter; one who works with stone or brick.

master-in-chancery: an assistant judge who heard cases and made recommendations to the judge of the chancery court.

master mariner: the commander of a ship.

master of the rolls: an equity judge.

Master Title Plat System: plats on which are shown survey data necessary to identify and describe public domain lands. The activity shown by the surveys indicate whether the availability of public land and resources need to be limited or restricted for use.

mater: (*Lat.*) mother, matron.

matefta magna: (*Lat.*) grandmother's sister (grand aunt).

matedera: (*Lat.*) mother's sister; aunt.

matria: (*Lat.*) mother.

matron: a married woman with children, especially an older woman; a woman in charge of a hospital or prison; a guard in such an institution.

matross: a private in the artillery or an assistant to the gunner.

mattock: a toot used for digging shaped like a pick-ax with a fiat blade on both sides.

maug: (*obsolete*) a close male connection, such as a brother-in-law or son-in-law.

Maundy Thursday: the Thursday before Good Friday.

maximus natu: (*Lat.*) eldest; first born.

meader: mower.

Mead Month: in the Republican calendar, July.

meander line: in surveying, a traverse of the line of a permanent natural body of water.

Mecklenburg Declaration of Independence: a document signed on 31 May 1775 by the prominent citizens of Mecklenburg, North Carolina declaring their independence from the British colonies in America.

medicine peddler: an itinerant salesman who dealt in herbs, elixers, pills, etc. which were bought in large batches and sold under his own label.

medicus: (*Lat.*) physician.

meeting seeds: seeds of dill fed to children during church services to dull the senses and keep them quieter.

melanuric: "malarial fever, black-water fever."—*Oxford English Dictionary*

meliorist: the belief that the world is moving naturally to a better state and that man can help in a positive way.

membranous croup: diphtheria.

menage: the members of a domestic establishment or household.

menage-man: an itinerant vendor who sells goods to be paid for in installments.

menagogue: a medicine that promotes menstrual flux.

meningitis: inflammation of the membranes of the brain or spinal cord.

men of straw: those who gave false evidence in court.

mensa et thoro: divorce; having to do with divorce.

mensis: (*Lat.*) month.

mercer: a person who deals in costly fabrics, especially silks.

merchant adventurer: [*also* merchant venturer] a member of an association of merchants who are incorporated by royalty or other authority to trade overseas and set up factories and trading stations in other countries.

mesne conveyance: a deed which intervenes between the original grant and the deed held by present owner—in some counties of Southern states these are filed in a separate mesne office.

mesne lord: in English law, a lord who obtained lands from the King and then gave others beneath his rank the right to use those lands.

mesne profit: rent and profit taken from land that a person has no legal right to use and who does not give it to the rightful owner.

messenger: 1: (*Plymouth Colony*) a constable. 2: (*England*) one who is appointed by a court to handle certain duties in a bankruptcy case.

messer: [*also* messour] an officer in a manor who acted as overseer at harvest time and was compensated by a portion of the profits.

Messidor: in the Republican calendar, the month of harvesting.

messour: *see* messer.

messuage: dwelling house.

mestizo: a person with one American Indian parent and one of Spanish or Portuguese descent.

meterer: a poet.

metes: the measurements of direction in seconds, minutes, and degrees plus the measurements of distance in feet, rods, poles, chains, miles, etc.

metes and bounds: [*also* courses and distances] a method of surveying property which made use of the natural physical and topographical features in conjunction with measurements and artificially designated objects or places— metes refers to the measuring of direction and distance while bounds refers to natural or man-made features on the land.

metreza: a mistress.

mews: stables grouped along a lane or an open courtyard.

miasma: poisonous vapor formerly supposed to arise from decomposing animal or vegetable matter, swamps, etc., and infect the air.

Michaelmas: a feast day, 29 September, on which rents and rates were due and a day on which many agreements and tenancies were dated.

middling fort: the relatively comfortable middle section of the county community.

midshipman: usually, a wealthy second or third son who could not inherit.

midwife: a woman experienced in the birthing process who helps other women in the birth of a child.

migrant: a person who changes a residence or habitat.

miles: (*Lat.*) knight; soldier.

milice: militia.

Military Company of Massachusetts: *see* Ancient and Honorable Artillery Company of Massachusetts.

military land: public land which was reserved as bounty land for soldiers of the Revolutionary War and War of 1 812, as part of their compensation for service.

Military Order of Foreign Wars of the United States: a group organized in 1894 for former, present, and future commissioned officers who served in a war or conflict with a foreign power, or in honorable service as an officer in the armed forces of U.S. allies, and for descendants in the direct male line from an officer.

Military Order of the Crusaders: a group organized in 1934 for males lineally descended from Crusaders of the rank of knight or more in the Crusades of 1096 to 1291 (membership by invitation only).

Military Order of the Loyal Legion of the United States: a group organized in 1865 for male lineal descendants of commissioned officers who served in the Union forces, from 1861 to 1865.

Military Society of the Mexican War: *see* Aztec Club of 1847.

Military Society of the War of 1812: an organization founded in 1790 (225 members) for the descendants of those who served in the American Revolution and the War of 1812.

milk fever: a fever accompanying the first flowing of milk in females after childbirth.

milk sickness: a rare disease, once common in the western United States, caused by drinking the milk, eating milk products, or flesh of cattle that have eaten any of various poisonous weeds.

mill: the tenth part of a cent, or the thousandth part of a dollar—used in calculating taxes, assessments, etc., but not as a coin.

miller: one who owns or operates a flour mill.

milleress: miller's wife.

mill lodge: a mill pond.

millpeck: one who sharpens mill stones.

mill pick: an iron tool used for giving millstones their corrugated or otherwise roughened surface.

mill pond: water held in a reservoir above a mill used to power the mill wheel.

mill race: the stream of water or the channel that carries the water to the mill wheel.

mill stone: large stones which rub together to grind grain.

mill tail: the water and/or the channel in which the water runs away from the mill wheel.

mill wheel: the water wheel which powers the machinery in a mill.

millwright: one who plans and builds mills or mill machinery.

minima natu: (*Lat.*) youngest.

ministerial act: *see* act.

minoris: (*Lat.*) lesser; younger.

mint master: 1: the person in charge of a mint. 2: one who invents or fabricates.

miscegenation: marriage of a man and woman who are different races.

misericord: 1: formerly, a relaxation of the strict rules in a monastery. 2: a ledge on the underside of a hinged seat that allowed a person to rest while standing. 3: a thin dagger used to kill mortally wounded knights.

Misericordia: a moveable feast day, the second Sunday after Easter.

misnomer: mistake in a person's name for identification purposes.

mistery: a trade or occupation.

mittimus: a writ ordering an authority to send or keep a person in prison.

mixer: bartender.

modius: ancient Roman corn measure equaling sixteen sextarii (somewhat less than two gallons).

mogul: 1: a powerful and important person, especially one who is prominent in a particular field. 2: a powerful steam locomotive used to pull other trains.

moiety: one half or equal share of anything.

moneyage: a general land tax levied by the two first Norman kings of England which consisted of a shilling on each hearth.

money-schrivener: a person who raises money for others.

monition: a summons from a higher court to a lower court to send documents or information.

monkshood: a medicinal plant; wolfsbane.

month's mind: a memorial service for one who has died, performed a month after the death.

moothall: a town hall.

mopsey: a puppet made of cloth.

moraine: a mound or small hill of dirt, rock, etc., that has been pushed up near the foot or side of a glacier.

Moravian: Protestants who organized in Bohemia in 1457. In 1734, after finding refuge in England, a party sailed for America settling in Pennsylvania. In 1752 a group settled in North Carolina.

morbus: disease.

moreen: a strong material made of wool and cotton and used for curtains.

more or less: approximately—often counted in rectangular survey system land descriptions. It comes from the fact that all north-south range lines used to establish reference points in the system are not true north, causing some sections to contain less than 640 acres.

morgan: [*also* morgen] a Dutch measure of land, the amount one man or team of horses could plow in one morning; two and one-tenth acres.

morganatic marriage: a marriage between a man of high rank and a woman of low rank. A contract assures that neither the wife nor any of the offspring of the marriage will ever inherit the rank, title, or property of the man.

morgen: *see* morgan.

mormal: gangrene.

Mormon church: *see* the Church of Jesus Christ of Latter-day Saints.

morphew: a scurvy eruption on the body.

morphine: [*also* morphinism] a chronic intoxication due to the habitual use of morphine or of opium in some other form.

mors omnibus communis: (*Lat.*) death is common to all.

morte sua defungi: (*Lat.*) die natural death.

mortis: (*Lat.*) death; corpse.

mortis causa: (*Lat.*) in view of death.

mortmain: unlawful alienation of land to anyone who would not allow the land to be circulated or used. It was considered land put into a "dead hand" if it was given to a church, monastery, or large corporation which would tie the land up for years without use.

mossback: 1: one who hid himself to avoid conscription in the Confederate army during the Civil War. 2: a very conservative person or one who is behind the times.

moulder: one who makes moulds for casting or one who moulds clay into brick.

mountebank: one who mounts a bench or stage in the market or other public place, boasts of his skill in curing diseases, and vends medicines which he pretends are infallible remedies.

mourning article: funeral gift.

mourning piece: a pictorial representation of a tomb, intended as a memorial of the dead.

movables: personal property such as furniture, animals, food, clothing, etc., which can be carried from place to place and is in the possession and use of the owner.

muck worm: a miser.

mudboat: a "land raft" on runners pulled by a horse; a flat boat used to transport mud, especially dredgings.

mudlark: 1: one who cleans sewers. 2: a waif.

muggler: *see* pigman.

mulatto: the offspring of one white and one black parent—sometimes used, especially on census schedules, for Indians.

muleskinner: a mule driver.

muleteer: one who drives a team of mules.

mulier: a legitimate child or a married woman.

multure: duty taken by the proprietor of the mill in the form of a portion of the corn ground in the mill.

multurer: a miller.

muniment: documents showing that a person has legal rights to land, possessions, or other privileges.

muniment of title: all written evidence of title which can show proof of ownership.

murrain beef: spoiled meat.

musard: 1: a dreamer or absent-minded person. 2: a vagabond.

musiker: a musician.

muster: the gathering of troops for preview parades, practice, or service.

muster out: a discharge from military service.

mustifee: one-sixteenth black; a child born of an octoroon and a white.

mustifino: one-thirty-second black; a child born of a mustifee and a white.

mutual will: a will made by two or more persons, which becomes invalid if one of the parties revokes it.

myelitis: inflammation of the spinal cord or bone marrow.

myocarditis: inflammation of the muscular walls of the heart.

N

nabob: a very wealthy man.

nactus: (*Lat.*) born.

nail: a measure of land; a measure used for cloth, which equals 2 1/4 inches or the sixteenth part of a yard; a measure of weight used for wool, beef, etc.

naked: in law, invalid or lacking a necessary condition—a naked deed or contract.

nam: named.

naperer: a royal servant in charge of the table linen.

napery: the business of making linen or linen cloth in general; a storeroom for linen.

napier: naperer.

nata: (*Lat.*) daughter.

National Huguenot Society: a group organized in 1931 as the Federation of Huguenot Societies and replaced in 1951 by the National Huguenot Society (composed of many State Societies) for members of the Protestant faith, over 18 years old, and lineally descended from a Huguenot who emigrated to America or other countries between 1520 and 1787, or from a Huguenot who remained in France despite the persecution.

National Road: [*also* Cumberland Road] a road beginning in Cumberland, Maryland, in 1811 (after approval in 1806), which was to extend to Wheeling, West Virginia, funded by the Federal government from proceeds of public land sales, and which ceased to be useful due to talk of repair as early as 1816.

National Society, Children of the American Revolution: a group organized in 1895 with approval of the Daughters of the American Revolution for persons under the age of 22 who are lineal descendants of patriots of the American Revolution.

National Society, Daughters of Colonial Wars: a society organized as Daughters of Colonial Wars in 1917 and the National Society in 1932 for women (over 18) who are acceptable to the society and lineally descended from an ancestor who served the colonies between 1607 and 1775 (several military or civil offices are also acceptable for membership).

National Society, Daughters of the American Colonists: a society organized in 1921 for women who are citizens (over 18) and lineal descendants of an ancestor who was in civil or military service in any of the colonies prior to 4 July 1776.

National Society, Daughters of the American Revolution: a society organized in 1890 for women (over 18) who are descended from a man or woman who served in the Revolution as a sailor, soldier, or civil officer in one of the colonies or states. They could also be a recognized patriot, or have given material aid to one of the before mentioned persons. The applicant must be personally acceptable to the society.

National Society, Daughters of the Barons of Runnemede: a society organized in 1921 for women (over 18) of lineal descent from a baron who secured the Magna Charta in the meadow of Runnemede in 1215 (membership by invitation only).

National Society, Daughters of the Revolution of 1776: a society organized in 1891 as the National Society, Daughters of the Revolution, an offshoot of the National Society, Daughters of the American Revolution. In 1972 "of 1776" was added to its title for identification of the Revolution with which it is associated. For women over 18 who are direct descendants of an ancestor who was loyal to American independence, shown by the following: signing the Declaration of Independence; membership in the Continental Congress, the Congress, a legislature or a general court of a colony or state; or by serving in the civil, military, or naval corps of the thirteen colonies.

National Society of Americans of Royal Descent: a society organized in 1908 for adults of royal descent. Membership is based upon current colonial society membership, acquaintance with at least one member of the executive council, and be presented and seconded in writing (membership by invitation only).

National Society of Dames of the Court of Honor: a society organized 1821 for females of lineal descent from a colonial governor or commissioned officer during the American wars from 1607 to 1865 (membership by invitation).

National Society of Lords of the Maryland Manors: a society organized in 1938 for lineal descendants of the first Baron Baltimore or a colonist granted a manor prior to 1722 (membership by invitation).

National Society of Magna Charta Dames: a society founded in 1909 for females descended from Magna Charta Sureties of 1215 (membership by invitation).

National Society of New England Women: a society organized in 1895 for women over 18 who descend from an ancestor born in New England before the signing of the Constitution in 1789.

National Society of Old Plymouth Colony Descendants: a society organized in 1910 for persons descending from those who came into the old Plymouth Colony before 1641.

National Society of the Children of the American Colonists: a society organized in 1939 for any child (21 or younger) of lineal descent from a colonist who served prior to 4 July 1776.

National Society of the Colonial Dames of the XVII Century: a society founded in 1915 for women who are lineal descendants of persons who served in a civil or military capacity, and who lived in one of the British colonies before 1701 as a colonist or a descendant of one.

National Society of the Colonial Daughters of the Seventeenth Century: a society organized in 1896 for women lineally descended from an ancestor who served the colonies from 1607 to 1699 (membership by invitation only).

National Society of the Daughters of Founders and Patriots of America: a society organized in 1898 for women (over 18) descended through the paternal line of a colonist who settled between 1607 and 1687. Could descend from one who proved loyal to American independence, from 1775 to 1784, but not from a polygamous marriage.

National Society of the Daughters of Utah Pioneers: a society organized in 1910 for women (over 18) who are lineal descendants of a pioneer who came to Utah between 1847 and 10 May

1869, when the railroad was completed.

National Society of the Sons of the American Revolution: a society organized in 1889 for men (over 18) who are direct lineal descendants of a patriot who participated in the American Revolution.

National Society of the Sons of Utah Pioneers: a society organized in 1933 for men (age 18 or over) who have at least one ancestor who lived in Utah before the arrival of the railroad on 10 May 1869.

National Society, Sons and Daughters of the Pilgrims: a society organized in 1908 for lineal descendants of settlers of the colonies before 1700.

National Society, United States Daughters of 1812: a society organized in 1892 for women who can prove that they are of lineal descent from an ancestor who gave civil, military, or naval service to this country between 1784 and 1815.

National Society, Women Descendants of the Ancient and Honorable Artillery Company: a society organized in 1927 for women (over 18) who are lineal

descendants of a member of the AHAC (1637-1774) or of the General Court of Boston (1 638).

Nativitas B.V. Mariae: a fixed feast day, the Birth of the Virgin Mary, 8 September.

Nativatas Domini: a fixed feast day, Christmas Day, 25 December.

natural child: a child born to a couple who have either not been married or whose marriage has not been accepted by a recording agency.

natural guardian: guardian who is responsible for the health and well-being of a minor regardless of the resources of that minor, such as a parent and child relationship.

natus: (*Lat.*) birth; age; son; offspring.

Naval and Military Order of the Spanish-American War: a society founded in 1899 (260 members) for former commissioned officers of the United States armed forces who served in the Spanish-American War, and for enlisted men who served but were commissioned later.

nave: the central part of the body of a church which extends from the rail of the choir to the main entrance.

navegot: an auger.

navigator: a laborer digging canals and, later, railways.

neat cattle: bulls, oxen, cows; any ox-like animal.

neatery: a place where cattle are kept.

nece: niece.

necessary house: outhouse or toilet.

neckrosis: *see* necrosis.

necrology: associated with keeping record of deaths; a listing of obituaries, as in a newspaper.

necrosis: [*also* neckrosis] the death of tissue; mortification, especially of the bones.

nedeller: one who makes needles.

nee: born—used when identifying a married woman by her maiden name.

ne exeat: a writ restraining someone from leaving the country.

Nemacolin's Path: a colonial highway between the Potomac and Ohio rivers. *See* Braddock's Road

neme: uncle.

nephew: in addition to the common usage, it could also mean an illegitimate son of an ecclesiastic, a niece, or a male or female grandchild.

nephritic: a purgative medicine to relieve or cure disorders of the kidneys, particularly gravel or stone in the bladder.

nephritis: inflammation of the kidneys.

nephrosis: any degeneration of the kidney, without signs of inflammation, due to the failure of fluid to be passed on through the kidneys to the bladder for disposal.

nephrotomy: the operation of extracting a stone from the kidney.

nepos: (*Lat.*) grandson; nephew.

nepotis: (*Lat.*) grandson; nephew; descendant.

neptis: (*Lat.*) granddaughter.

netvine: a medicine for relief of nervous disorders.

Netherlands Society of Philadelphia: a society organized in 1892 for males of lineal descent from a Dutch ancestor born in America before 4 July 1776, or a Dutch immigrant after 1776.

neuralgia: an affection of one or more nerves causing intermittent but frequent pain.

neutral ground: unsettled area between Louisiana and Spanish Texas.

New Connecticut: *see* Western Reserve.

Newlander: European promoter hired by merchants and ship captains, beginning in the 1720s and 1730s, to go about Europe soliciting people of substance to become emigrants for the increasingly profitable trade of transporting redemptioners to America.

new mother: (*colonial America*) stepmother.

New Orleans boat: a very large flatboat used on the Ohio and Mississippi Rivers.

New Style calendar: the calendar initiated by Pope Gregory to replace the Old Style or Julian calendar. *See* Gregorian calendar.

New Year bread: *see* Marchpane.

next friend: one who acts on behalf of another person if they cannot act for themselves, such as a minor or an incompetent, when they have no legal guardian.

Nicholites: a religious group in Delaware in 1793.

niece: sometimes, granddaughter; *(pre-seventeenth-century England)* any descendant, male or female, and occasionally, any younger relative.

nigger: a steam-engine used on ships; a steam powered vehicle used in hauling river-boats over bars or snags.

night-magistrate: a constable.

nimgimmer: doctor, surgeon, or apothecary.

nine-ber: [*also* 9ber] in the Old Style calendar, November.

nippers: 1: handcuffs or leg irons. 2: a thief or pickpocket. 3: a small boy who is an assistant to a workman or costermonger.

nisi prius: a court that tries a case before a jury and a judge only instead of a full sitting of justices.

niter: [*also* saltpeter] potassium nitrate, used in gun powder making.

Nivose: in the Republican calendar, the month of snow.

nob-thatcher: one who made wigs.

nomen: (*Lat.*) name-family.

non-associator: a man who did not believe in fighting (a Quaker, Mennonite, etc.) associators were men who were willing to go to war. *See* associator.

non compos: (*Lat.*) of unsound mind.

non compos mentie: (*Lat.*) incompetent, or not mentally capable of handling one's affairs.

Non Conformist: a Protestant who refused to accept the ceremonies and doctrines of the Church of England; the English clergyman who refused to submit to the 1662 Set of Uniformity which required all English clergy submit to Episcopal reordination regardless of previous affiliation.

non est inventus: (*Lat.*) not found.

North American Manx Association: a group founded in 1928 by immigrants from the Isle of Man who include some of the early Plymouth and Virginia Company colonists, Revolutionary War soldiers, etc. Primary membership is composed of Manxmen and their spouses and descendants.

Northern Neck: [*also* Farfax propriety] the land situated between the Rappahannock and Potomac rivers extending westward to their head springs, being some 5,282,000 acres (present day West Virginia).

Northwest Ordinance of 1785: the Land Ordinance Act of 1785, which provided that public lands be surveyed and described with terms such as township, range, section and subsection (or any portion thereof).

NorthwestTerritory: a territory created in 1787 out of land ceded to the United States under the Treaty of Paris in 1783 in which most of the inhabitants were French.

nostrum: a panacea or quack medicine, the ingredients of which were kept secret.

noterer: (*obsolete*) a notary.

note-shaver: one who promotes phoney financial companies; a usurer.

nothus: (*Lat.*) spurious; illegitimate; a bastard.

notarial will: [*also* authentic will] authentic will made by the testator before a notary and retained by him until the death.

note of hand: promissory note.

nova nupta: (*Lat.*) bride.

noverca: (*Lat.*) stepmother.

novus: (*Lat.*) new; young; fresh.

novus maritus: (*Lat.*) bridegroom.

nubo: (*Lat.*) to marry (a husband).

nudum pactum: (*Lat.*) a contract or agreement that has no consideration on one side, making it unenforceable.

nulla bona: (*Lat.*) no goods.

nul tiel records: (*Lat.*) no such record.

nunc pro tunc: (*Lat.*) *literally* "now for then"; an act done now, which should have been done previously.

nuncupative will: [*also* oral will] a will, which to be valid, must be given by a person in their last hours, witnessed by two or more witnesses, and written within a period of six to twelve days (depending on laws in effect).

nunrye: (*obsolete*) a nunnery.

nupta: (*Lat.*) married (of a woman).

nuptiae: (*Lat.*) marriage.

nuptialis: (*Lat.*) nuptial.

nuptus: (*Lat.*) married.

nurus: (*Lat.*) daughter-in-law; young woman.

O

obelisk: a tall slender four sided pillar, tapering as it rises so the top resembles a pyramid; gravestone.

obiit: (*Lat.*) he/she died.

obiit codem anno: (*Lat.*) died the same year.

obiit repentina morte: (*Lat.*) died without sacrament (suddenly).

obiit sine prole: (*Lat.*) he/she died without issue.

obiit sine prole masculus: (*Lat.*) he/she died without male issue.

obiit vitra patris: (*Lat.*) died in the lifetime of his or her father.

obit: a mass or service for the soul of a deceased person observed on the anniversary of his death; death; a funeral ceremony.

obit eodem anno: (*Lat.*) [*also* obit endam anno] died the same year.

obiter: (*Lat.*) incidentally.

obiter dicta: (*Lat.*) last words.

oblation: an offering; a present.

occupier: a tradesman.

ochre: iron ore, often earthy and impure, used for making paints.

octavo: the page size of a book made up of printer's sheets folded into leaves.

octoroon: a person having one-eighth black ancestry, such as a child of a quadroon and a white.

Oculi: a moveable feast day, the third Sunday in Lent, the fourth before Easter.

of color: a black, Indian, or person of mixed blood.

Ohio Company's Purchase: about 1,000,000 acres lying along the Ohio River. Tract purchased by Manasseh Cutler and Winthrop Sargeant, agents for the Ohio Company. First permanent settlement made under the ordinance of 1787 was made at Marietta in 1788.

Ohio Land Grants: *see* Fire Lands.

Ohio packet boat: a large boat, 75 to 100 feet long and 15 to 20 feet wide, which made the run between Pittsburgh and Cincinnati and Louisville.

Old Connecticut Path: an early colonial highway between Boston, Massachusetts and Albany, New York which traveled through the cities of Wayland, Marlborough, Worcester, Oxford, and Springfield, Massachusetts.

Old Dominion: Virginia.

Old Northwest Turnpike: a well-traveled highway which stretched from Winchester, Virginia, to the Ohio River at Parkersburg, West Virginia.

Old Southwest: the area of Tennessee and Kentucky, later included Alabama, Mississippi, and parts of Louisiana and Arkansas.

Old Style calendar: the Julian calendar, which was replaced by the Gregorian calendar.

Old Walton Road: an early route to the West from Knoxville to Nashville, Tennessee.

olographic will: *see* holographic will.

onkotomy: the opening of a tumor or abscess.

onset: farm dwelling, including the outhouses.

onstead: a single farmhouse with its attached stables, cowsheds, and other offices.

on sufferance: a poor family who relied on neighbors and the kindness of others for their sustenance.

open field: a system by which open farmland or pasture was divided among the villagers but not fenced off.

operarius: (*Lat.*) laborer.

opere citato: (*Lat.*) in the work cited.

ophthalmoscopy: (*archaic*) a branch of medical science which studies the knowledge of a man's temper and manner from the appearance of the eyes.

opiate: any medicine that induces sleep or respite; a narcotic.

opodoldoc: a camphorated liniment or soap solution in ardent spirits with camphor and other oils added.

oppeto: (*Lat.*) to go to meet; to perish; to die.

oppidanus: (*Lat.*) of or in a town (other than Rome).

optimas: (*Lat.*) aristocrat.

optimus: (*Lat.*) the best.

or: in heraldry, a gold or yellow color represented in engravings by dots upon a plain field.

oral will: *see* nuncupative will.

orator: a male petitioner or plaintiff.

oratorie: a private chapel or closet used for prayer.

oratory: a place of prayer, such as a small room or chapel attached to a house.

oratrix: a female petitioner or plaintiff.

orbitas: (*Lat.*) orphanage; widowhood.

orbo: (*Lat.*) to bereave (of parents, children, etc.).

orbus: bereaved; childless; parentless.

orderly: a non-commissioned officer or private in the military service assigned to look after the needs of superior officers or to carry orders or messages.

Order of Americans of Armorial Ancestry: a group founded in 1903 for anyone, 18 or over, who is of good moral character and who proves descent from an immigrant ancestor who had a proved right to bear arms in the country of his or her origin.

Order of Colonial Lords of Manors in America: a group established in 1911 for lineal descendants of the order's twenty-seven recognized patroons, lords of the manor, or seigniors (by invitation only).

Order of Descendants of Colonial Physicians and Chirurgeons: a group organized in 1974 for people descended from a physician, chirurgeon, or licensed midwife, practicing in North America before 1784 (membership by invitation).

Order of the Crusades, 1096-1192: a group organized in 1936 for persons of lineal descent from a participant in one of three Crusades from 1096-1192 (membership by invitation only).

Order of First Families of Virginia: a group organized in 1912 for those lineal descendants of ancestors who helped establish the Virginia Colony (membership by invitation).

Order of Stars and Bars: a group organized in 1938 for males of lineal or collateral descent from commissioned officers of the Confederate States of America.

Order of the Crown in America: a group organized in 1898 for those of proven royal descent, with women being required to be members of the Colonial Dames of America or National Society of Colonial Dames of America (by invitation only).

Order of the Crown of Charlemagne in the United States of America: a group organized in 1939 for men and women who are lineally descended from the Emperor Charlemagne (membership by invitation).

Order of the First Families of Mississippi, 1699-1817: a group organized in 1967 for lineal descendants of those who resided in Mississippi between 1699 and statehood in 1817.

Order of the Founders and Patriots of America: a group organized in 1896 for male citizens (over 18) of good reputation and lineal descent, in the male line, of a pre-1657 colonist and a descendant (same surname) who served as a patriot during the Revolutionary War.

Order of Washington: a group reorganized in 1895 for persons of lineal descent from one of the patriots whose lineage and loyalty to the cause of the Colonists is a matter of record. The ancestor must have arrived in America prior to 1750, have been a landowner and civil or church official, and also have had a male descendant who assisted the colonies.

order of admission: *see* admission.

ordinary: 1: an ecclesiastical judge; in the United States (some states), a judicial officer with authority to rule in matters of probate. 2: a public house where meals were served to the community. 3: in heraldry, any one of the major devices used as heraldic distinctions.

Oregon Compromise: a treaty with Britain in 1846 which allowed the United States to add the area containing the states of Oregon, Washington, and Idaho.

orfever: a goldsmith.

origo: (*Lat.*) beginning; birth; origin.

oriundus: (*Lat.*) descended; spring from.

orphan asylum: orphanage.

Orphan Cars: the train or car which carried orphan children to new homes.

Orphan Chamber: the chamber or court presided over by the orphan master which deals with minors, wills, etc.

Orphan's Court: in Pennsylvania, the court which handled probate matters.

Orphan Trains: the trains that took children (from 1854 to 1929) who had been placed by Children's Aid Societies to new homes where they would live and work.

ortus: (*Lat.*) rising; sunrise; birth.

ossification: the formation of bone; the process of becoming or changing into bone; the condition of being ossified.

osteopath: 1: professional person required to buy a permit or license thus contributing through indirect tax. 2: one who practices osteopathy.

osteopathy: a theory of disease and method of cure based on the assumption that loss of structural integrity of the skeleton is the cause of most diseases.

osteo sarcoma: a disease or sarcoma of the bony tissue, characterized by a fleshy growth.

ostery: (*obsolete*) hostry; hostess.

ostreger: [*also* ostringer] a keeper of goshawks.

otitis: inflammation of the ear.

ousen: (*obsolete*) oxen.

out-crier: an auctioneer.

outlet: an animal not housed during the winter or during the night.

out-lots: lots outside of the boundaries of a village used for pasture or farming.

outsettier: one who makes his home at some distance from the main body of the town or village.

over-roller: a roller pulled by oxen or horses to flatten snow.

owlet: a smuggler of sheep and/ or wool out of England.

oxgang: as much land as an ox could plow in a year, approximately 15 to 20 acres.

Oyer andTerminer: high courts of criminal jurisdiction.

P

paage: a toll paid to a land owner for permission to pass over his lands.

pace: a measure of distance, two and one-half to 3 feet.

packers: one who packs goods for preservation, such as pickles or herring.

Paddington Fair: a name used for an execution because of the common use of the English parish of Paddington for this purpose.

paduasoy: a rich smooth silk originally made in Padua.

page: boy-servant; a youth training for knighthood.

painter: a rope attached to the bow of a ship used to fasten it to a dock, buoy, or another ship.

Palatinate: the area in Germany known as Der Pfalz. *See* Palatine.

Palatine: one who is a native of the Palatinate area called Der Pfalz, literally the old south and west kingdoms of Germany—the American interpretation has come to include all early German immigrants.

pale: 1: in heraldry, an ordinary (an object placed upon the field); a vertical band in the center of the shield occupying one third of the field. 2: an enclosure or boundary; limit.

paleography: study of handwriting, usually that of original records.

palfrey: an ordinary riding horse; a small saddle horse used by women.

palimpsest: a parchment, tablet, etc., which has been written on one or more times.

paling man: one who deals in eels.

palliard: a lecher; a vagabond.

palsy: the loss or defect of the power of voluntary muscular motion in all or part of the body; paralysis.

panacea: a universal remedy for all diseases.

pancake bell: bell rung on Shrove Tuesday after English

Catholics had confessed their sins and would traditionally dine on pancakes.

pandemic: occurring over a wide geographic area and affecting an exceptionally high proportion of the population.

pannier: 1: a wicker basket used for carrying loads on a mule or horse. 2: a skirt puffed out at the sides. 3: a shield behind which medieval archers crouched.

pannier man: 1: one who hawks fish. 2: one who conveys his goods to market in panniers.

panoply: a full suit of armor.

panter: [*also* panterer] keeper of the pantry.

pantile-shop: a meeting house.

pantier: a butler.

Papist: a Roman Catholic.

parage: 1: (*obsolete*) birth or parentage. 2: equality of birth or estate.

parcel: a piece of land with definite boundaries and a specific description.

parcener: one or more persons who hold an estate by virtue of descent, generally known as an estate in coparcenary, and refers to the estate before the inheritance has been divided.

parchment: writing material made from the skin of an animal, usually a sheep or goat; paper with a texture that resembles parchment.

pardoner: a cleric authorized to grant or sell ecclesiastical pardons, or indulgences, in the Roman Catholic Church.

paregoric: a camphoreted tincture of opium that soothes or lessens pain.

patens: (*Lat.*) father, mother; parents.

parent county: the county from which a new one is formed.

parentlie: kindred.

parentis: (*Lat.*) father; mother; parents.

parento: (*Lat.*) 1: to offer a sacrifice in honor of deceased

parento: (*Lat.*) 1: to offer a sacrifice in honor of deceased parents or relatives. 2: to take revenge for a person's death by killing another.

paring plow: a plow used for cutting sod or turf from the surface of the ground.

pari passu: (*Lat.*) in equal degree; with equal speed.

parishing: a hamlet or small village belonging to a parish.

parity of hands: specimens of handwriting which are compared and proved to be the same.

parker: one who keeps a park; a caretaker.

paroch: (Lat.) a parish clergyman.

parol: by word of mouth; evidence given orally rather than written.

paroxysm: a fit of higher excitement or emotion in a disease; convulsion.

parrot's bill: a surgeon's pincers.

partition: a division of land when two or more persons hold real estate as co-tenants, and then each take separate parts.

partition of a succession: a division of effects, in which a succession is composed among all the co-heirs according to their respective rights which may be voluntary or judicial.

parturition: childbirth.

parva: (*Lat.*) little.

parvenu: a person of vague origin who has suddenly accumulated a large amount of wealth but who lacks social standing.

parvis: an enclosed area in front of a church.

Pasch: Easter Sunday; the first Sunday after the full moon on or after 21 March.

pasquinade: publicly posted satirical writing.

pass: announcing the death of a person by tolling a bell.

passim: (*Lat.*) here and there; far and wide in a disorderly manner; throughout.

passing bell: a bell which is tolled to indicate the death of someone.

Passing Meeting: in the records of the Society of

Friends (Quakers), a statement added to a marriage entry when the couple had been married by the prescribed method.

pasteler: [*also* pasterer; paster] a pastry maker.

pastor: a shepherd or herdsman.

pastoral acts: the acts, such as baptism, confirmation, marriage, etc., performed by a pastor of a congregation or a bishop of a diocese. *See* act.

patache: a small boat used in carrying men or orders from one ship or place to another.

patent: [*also* letters patent] a grant made by a government to an individual, conveying fee-simple title to public lands; the official document of such a grant; the land so granted.

patentee: one who receives a grant of land byway of a patent.

pater: (*Lat.*) father; sire.

pater familias: (*Lat.*) head of a household; father of a family.

patres: (*Lat.*) father.

patroller: local (county) court appointed official.

patron: 1: the captain of a small vessel. 2: one who grants church benefices.

Patrons of Husbandry: [*also* Grange] an organization established by farmers of the United States in 1867 whose object was to bring together the producers and consumers of farm and factory products in an attempt to do away with the services of middlemen and speculative traders.

patronymic: in strict usage, a name formed by the addition of a prefix or suffix indicating sonship or other relationship to the name of one's father or paternal ancestor, as Johnson (son of John), Macdonald (son of Donald), etc.

patroon: under old Dutch government of New York, one who owned a landed estate and had certain manorial privileges.

patruelis: (*Lat.*) cousin on the father's side.

patruus: (*Lat.*) paternal uncle.

patuus major: (*Lat.*) grandfather's brother; grand uncle.

pattens: [*also* pattoons] a thick soled platform attached to everyday shoes worn in bad weather on muddy roads.

pauper: a person who has become so poor that he cannot take care of himself and is reliant on the government to support him.

pavage: a toll assessed for crossing the land of someone else, i.e., purchasing the right to trespass.

pavia: in medieval warfare, a large shield used for protection.

paviser: a soldier who carried a pavis.

peager: a toll-keeper; a toll assessed for passing through a particular place.

peavy: [*also* peavey] a cant-hook with a spike on the end of the lever used by a lumberman.

peculiar: a piece of land not incorporated in a township.

peculiar jurisdiction: in canon law, a jurisdiction not subject to the bishop of a diocese.

peculium: (*Lat.*) private property of a son, daughter, or slave with the father's or master's permission.

pecuniary: relating to money; involving a fine.

pedagogue: 1: a teacher. 2: (*ancient Greece*) a slave who would take care of children and sometimes act as a tutor.

pedaile: a footman; a foot soldier.

pedant: a teacher, one who is strict about obeying a set of arbitrary rules.

peddler: a person who travels from place to place selling small goods.

peeler: a policeman, named after Sir Robert Peel who established the Irish police force and reorganized the London force.

peer: a person belonging to one of the five degrees of nobility (duke, marquis, earl, viscount, baron) in England.

peerage: rank of nobleman; a book or list of peers with their lineage.

pellex: (*Lat.*) concubine (of a married man).

pemphigus: a skin disease characterized by the formation of watery blisters.

pennyroyal: a species of mint, formerly much cultivated and valued for its medicinal virtues.

Pentecost: a moveable feast day, Whitsunday, the seventh Sunday after Easter, ending the Easter season.

pepaatic: a medicine that serves to help digestion.

peppercorn: the dried berry of a black pepper, which was used in Old England as a token payment of rent.

perambulation: [*also, in United States* procession] a process used in England to reaffirm or preserve land boundaries. *See* procession.

perambulator: a surveyor; the instrument used by surveyors which rolls over the ground and measures distance.

per annum: (*Lat.*) by the year, annually.

perch: a unit of land measure equal to a rod or pole (16.5 feet or 5.5 yards).

peregrinator: a traveler who wanders about in foreign countries.

peregrinus: (*Lat.*) strange; stranger; foreigner.

pericarditis: inflammation of the sac around the heart.

periodic tenancy: a tenancy which may be terminated by a written notice, a month to month, for example.

peripatetic: itinerant philosopher.

peripneumonia: inflammation of the lungs.

perishables: the part of an estate which may diminish or disappear, between the date the will is probated and the expected final settlement, such as livestock, crops, etc.

peritonitis: inflammation of the peritoneum, the membrane which lines the abdominal cavity, usually the most serious complication of appendicitis.

perfugue: [*also* peruke; peruque] a wig.

perruguier: [*also* peruker; perukier] a wig maker.

per se: (*Lat.*) by itself; in itself.

personalty: personal property; any goods or properties that are moveable.

per stirpes: (*Lat.*) [*also* in stirpes] distribution of an inheritance by giving equal shares to family groups rather than an equal percentage to each descendant.

per testes: (*Lat.*) by witnesses.

pertussis: *see* whooping cough.

peseta: *see* pistoroen.

pessoner: a fishmonger.

pesthouse: a house or hospital for persons infected with a contagious disease.

petechial fever: a small red or purple spot in the skin occurring in certain fevers.

peterman: a fisherman.

petit: small, as in a petit court or small claims court.

petit jury: [*also* trial jury] a six to twelve member jury.

petit larceny: the stealing of goods valued at twelve pence or less, as opposed to grand larceny.

petit treason: the crime of killing a person to whom the offender owes duty or subjection—a wife killing her husband, a servant his master, etc.

pettifogger: a small time lawyer retained by a small or mean business.

pew fellow: a companion.

pharmacopoeist: a person who sells medicines; an apothecary.

phebotomia: *see* fleam.

phlebotomy: the act of opening a vein for letting blood.

phrenitis: formerly inflammation of the brain, with acute fever and delirium; inflammation of the diaphragm.

phrenologist: a person who studies the shape and protuberances of the skull and makes an analysis of the character and development of this person's faculties.

phthiriasis: infestation of lice.

phthisis: a progressive wasting away of the body, such as tuberculosis, pulmonary consumption, etc.

physick: the art or science of healing by the use of medicines and therapeutics, especially with a cathartic to cleanse the body.

picaroon: a pirate or a pirate's ship; a thief, adventurer, or rogue.

picayune: a coin with little value; anything small or considered worthless.

pickeer: to pillage or steal cattle; to skirmish.

pieces of eight: a Spanish or Spanish-American silver dollar with the value of eight reals.

pie plant: rhubarb.

Piepoudre, Court of: when a fair or market was held the steward or parson in charge was given permission to have a court to maintain order. The steward headed the court with the market traders being the jury and dealt with such cases as fair measure, bad or inferior goods, assault, and pilfering—the name of the court was thought to have come from a French word, pieds poudreux, meaning dusty feet, which was a nickname for an Itinerant peddler.

piggin: a small drinking vessel, such as a wooden dipper or pail, with a long handle.

pigman: [*also* muggler] a seller of crockery.

pike: a highway on which the maintenance is obtained through a toll paid by those who travel the road.

pikeman: a miller's assistant.

pilled: 1: plundered or robbed. 2: sparse head of hair; bald.

piller: a robber.

pillery: pillage; robbery.

pillion: a small cushion attached to the back of a saddle allowing another person to ride, usually a woman.

pillory: a form of punishment whereby the person was put in wooden stocks, with the hands and head confined, and left for a period of time in public.

pillowbeer: [*also* pillowbere; pillowber] pillow case.

pilot: one licensed to steer ships through difficult waters.

pinchbeck: 1: an inferior metal of copper and zinc used in making cheap jewelry. 2: later, anything cheap or imitation.

pinder: a person whose duty is to catch and confine stray animals.

pine mast violations: the cutting down of white pine trees of about 24" diameter and at least thirty feet high which were reserved for the king for his ship's masts, for which one could be punished.

piner: 1: a pioneer. 2: a laborer.

pin money: an annual sum given to a woman by her husband for her personal expenses such as clothing and other small items.

pipe: a cask used for wine, oil, etc., with a volume of 126 gallons.

piper: an innkeeper.

pirouqe: a boat resembling a canoe in shape, made by hollowing out a log.

Piscataqua Pioneers: a group organized in 1905 for descendants of the original settlers who lived on the sides of the Piscataqua River (Maine/New Hampshire border) before the signing of the Declaration of Independence.

piscator: (*Lat.*) fisherman.

pistoroen: [*also* peseta] a small Spanish coin.

pitancer: a person in a religious house who distributed pittances.

pit and gallows: punishment by hanging or drowning.

pitman: a coal miner; one who works in a pit.

pityriasis: a condition of the skin characterized by the formation and falling off of scales; dandruff.

placing-out: programs to Place children in homes where they could receive education and care in exchange for labor.

plain people: religious groups from the Palatinate, Mennonites, Dunkards, Moravians, Schwenkfelders, etc.

plank road: a road made with timbers laid lengthwise on the road bed, and flooring planks laid transversely across the timbers, to accommodate heavy loads.

plastering hair: hair obtained from animals or humans (barber shop sweepings), mixed in with plaster, and spread on walls.

pleading: paper filed with the court by the parties in a litigation stating the basis for legal action.

pleurisy: an inflammation of the pleura (membrane) that covers the inside of the thorax, accompanied with fever, pain, and cough.

plough jogger: a plowman.

plow-alms: money which every plow-land was required of every plow land to be given to the church, usually a penny.

plow-bote: in English law, the allowed amount of wood given to each tenant for the repair of his farm equipment.

plow foot: a rod attached to a plow used to adjust the depth at which the ground was plowed.

plow land: as much land as could be plowed by a team of eight oxen in a year.

plowman: a farm worker; a husbandman.

plowright: one who makes or repairs plows.

plumbum: lead.

plumbum man: a plumber; one who works with lead pipe.

plumper: a small piece of ivory or other object carried in the mouth to plump up cheeks or fill where teeth had been extracted.

plumlist: one who holds two or more offices of benefices at the same time.

Pluviose: in the Republican calendar, the month of rain.

pocosin: *see* poquoson.

podagra: gout in the feet.

poke-bag: a small purse.

poke bonnet: a bonnet, often worn by Quaker women, that had a wide brim that stuck out beyond the face.

pokerwork: burning designs onto a light colored wood with a heated pointed implement.

polail: poultry.

pole: a unit of measure equal to a rod or perch (16.5 feet or 5.5 yards).

pole axe: a long handled battle-ax which has a spike, hook, or hammer opposite the blade.

poleman: a surveyor's assistant.

polentier: [*also* poltaire; polter] a poulterer; an officer in charge of poultry in the king's kitchen.

poler: an extortioner.

poliomyelitis: [*also* infantile paralysis; polio] an inflammation of the anterior horn cells in the gray matter of the spinal cord.

poll: 1: the head, specifically the part where hair grows. 2: a register or list of individuals who are liable for payment of a head tax.

pollage: 1: a head tax. 2: extortion; robbery.

poll tax: a tax levied on people rather than on property—often a tax on those voted, and only those who paid the tax could vote, thus it was an effort to keep the poor or undesirables from voting.

poltroon: a craven coward.

pony homestead: a tax exemption granted to heads of households on household goods to the amount of $300.

populus: (*Lat.*) people.

poquoson: [*also* pocosin] a swamp or overflowed land.

portage: a fee for transportation of goods.

porter: 1: a beer made from charred or browned malt. 2: a pallbearer. 3: a doorman.

porterage: a fee charged by porters for carrying another's baggage.

porterhouse: an inn or tavern where beer, porter, etc., was sold.

portmantle: [*also* portmanteau] a leather bag used for traveling.

post: 1: after. 2: to announce. 3: to register something with a public official.

posthumous child: a child born after the death of the father.

postilion: a man who waited for coaches and wagons to help them up steep hills by attaching extra horses.

postman and tubman: in England, an experienced barrister in the Court of Exchequer.

post mill: a windmill built on a vertical axis so that it could be turned as the direction of the wind changes.

post mortem: after death—such as the removal of a body from a grave.

post-natus: (*Lat.*) *literally* "born afterwards"; a person born after a particular historic event, and whose status or rights are governed by the timing of his or her birth relative to that event.

post rider: one who carries mail over a post road.

post ridie: (*Lat.*) on the day after; the next day.

potboiler: [*also* potwaller; potwalloper] in some English boroughs, before the Reform Act of 1832, a man who qualified for a parliamentary vote as a householder, i.e., tenant of a house or distinct part of one, as distinguished from one who was merely a member or inmate of a householder's family.

pothouse: a disreputable tavern or alehouse.

pottage: a thick soup made of meat and vegetables.

potter: one who makes or peddles pottery or earthenware vessels.

potter's asthma: a form of fibroid phthisis to which persons exposed to the dust of the pottery industry are subject.

potter's field: a burial place for the poor and homeless.

pottle: a pot or tankard having the capacity of one-half gallon.

potwaller: a potboiler; a specific class of voters. *See* potboiler.

potwalloper: *see* potboiler.

poulter: one who deals in poultry.

poultice: a soft, hot, moist substance as of flour, meal, bran, flax seed, or similar substances, applied to sores or inflamed parts of the body.

pound: an English unit of money, twenty shillings or 100 new pennies.

powder monkey: a boy who carried gunpowder from the magazine to the guns on a man-of-war.

praecipe: a written order to the clerk of a court to issue a writ or action not required to be presented before the judge in open court.

praedial land: [*also* predial land] property attached to land, such as slaves; issuing or coming from the land, such as tithes.

praedium: (*Lat.*) lands; estate.

praenomen: (*Lat.*) first name.

Prairial: in the Republican calendar, the month of meadows.

prebend: a source of income possessed by some collegiate and cathedral churches a prebendary was an official appointed to receive such an income.

precinct: county subdivision in Idaho, Illinois, Washington, and Wyoming, similar to a ward, providing police protection, court justice, and such services.

precisian: a sixteenth- or seventeenth-century Puritan; one who is very precise in his observance of religious rites.

predial land: *see* praedial land.

predicator: preacher; a preaching friar.

Preemption Act: in 1841, a permanent preemption act which allowed anyone who was the head of a family (including widows), or over 21 and a U.S. citizen, or who had declared intention to become one, to stake a claim on any tract up to 160 acres and then buy it from the government for $1.25 per acre.

preemption lands: public lands previously granted by another sovereign.

prentis: an apprentice.

prepositor: a senior student in an English public school with the authority to discipline.

presbyter: one who has the pastoral care of a particular church; (*Saxon*) mass-palest.

prescription: the right to use a particular piece of land; a right, or title through possession and continual use.

presentment: a record of a person who is brought before a court to answer charges in a criminal matter.

presents: "'this document or instrument"; used in legal documents to indicate the document in which the phrase is mentioned, "by these presents."

presidio: Spanish military post and/or a district in the Spanish Southwest.

press gang: a group of men employed by a ship's captain to press men into service or as workers on a ship.

press-money: money paid to a man impressed into public service.

prestidigitator: a magician; a juggler; one who juggles words.

pretermit: to leave out a particular heir from a will.

pricker: 1: a light horseman. 2: a witch-finder.

pricking aches: see aches.

pricking note: a bill of goods for shipment, on which a customs officer noted or pricked each item as it came on board.

pricking wheel: a small wheel with sharp teeth on the outside edge used by a saddler for marking holes for stitches; a tracing wheel used by seamstresses.

prick louise: (obsolete) contemptuously, a tailor.

pridem: (Lat.) long since.

pridie: (Lat.) on the day before.

prig-napper: a horse thief.

prima facie: (Lat.) literally "at first sight"; something which at first view of the matter gives enough evidence to establish it as fact without further searching.

primage: hat money; a small percentage added to the freight charge and given to the owner; a small fee paid to the crew and captain of a ship by the shipper for loading and unloading cargo.

primer-fine: in England, a fee given the King at the beginning of a suit by fine.

primogeniture: an old common-law system of inheritance whereby the oldest son inherited the father's property, excluding all other sons or daughters.

principal meridian: the first or beginning north-south running line laid out in each of thirty-seven different surveys in public domain states of the United States.

priores: (*Lat.*) ancestors.

prisage: the custom of the crown of England to take two tons of wine from every ship importing twenty tons or more.

privateer: a privately owned sea vessel carrying special papers, called letters of Marque and Reprisal, authorizing it to capture enemy vessels (prizes) at sea and present them to the prize session of an admiralty court for condemnation.

Privy Council: the governing body in early Virginia which authorized various acts (programs of settlement for the crown), such as a method of distributing land called the headright system, as well as passing colonial laws and so on.

privigne: (*Lat.*) stepdaughter.

privignus: (*Lat.*) stepson.

privity: in law, a relationship to, or mutual interest in, the same property.

privy: in law, one of the interested parties.

Prize Court: a special session of the Admiralty Court held only during wartime which deter-mined what should happen to captured enemy ships (prizes). *See* Admiralty Court.

pro: (*Lat.*) for.

pro anno: (*Lat.*) for the year.

proavia: (*Lat.*) great-grandmother.

proavus: (*Lat.*) great-grandfather; ancestor.

probang: in surgery, an instrument of whalebone and sponge used for removing obstructions in the throat.

probationer: students of divinity who teach in several different locations.

procession: [*also, in England* perambulate] the process of re-establishing land ownership boundaries by physically walking them in company with an appointed processioner and the owners of the adjoining lands.

processioner: a court-appointed official whose job was to mark off and verify a disputed boundary line.

prochein ami: (*Lat.*) *literally* "next friend"; one who acts for the benefit of a minor without being appointed until an official guardian can be found.

proclamation money: 1: the money paid to a person as part of the freedom dues which were received upon completion of an indenture or apprenticeship. 2: (*colonial America*) foreign coins and rated commodities.

proctor: 1: one who represents another person's cause in a civil or ecclesiastical court. 2: magistrate of a university.

professional mourner: one paid to mourn at a funeral or wake.

progenies: (*Lat.*) face; family; progeny.

progenitology: the search for progenitors, reasoning that genealogy, according to the dictionary, deals with the searching and recording of descent, not ancestry.

progeny: the issue or descendants of a common ancestor.

pro hac vice: (*Lat.*) for this one particular occasion.

proles: (*Lat.*) offspring; progeny; descendants.

promiscuous entry: listing a person in the order he became related to the church, meaning in random or mixed order.

promotor: an informer; in an ecclesiastical court, the plaintiff in a suit.

pronepos: (*Lat.*) great-grandson.

proneptis: (*Lat.*) great-granddaughter.

pronurus: (*Lat.*) wife of a grandson.

proof of heirship: a proceeding which produces documents establishing the heirs and providing degrees of relationship, especially when a will is being contested.

proof of residence: in the naturalization process, the paperwork, usually an affidavit, verifying the length of residency (3-5 years) of an alien in the U.S. as fulfillment of a requirement to become a citizen.

propinquity: a kinship with or for; nearness of relationship; kinship.

propositus: 1: one from whom a line of descent is traced. 2: an ancestor intestate.

propounder: one who puts before the court a motion for consideration to proceed with probate.

prosapia: (*Lat.*) family; pedigree; race.

prostatitis: inflammation of the prostrate gland.

pro tempore: (*Lat.*) temporarily.

prothonotary: chief notary or law clerk; a registrar or head of a court.

protocol: an original document or record of a transaction.

proved: documents such as wills, deeds, bills of sale, etc., having their accuracy and honesty attested to through legal proceedings in a court of law.

provenance: an archival arrangement or listing of documents.

provender: dry food for livestock; fodder.

provis: provision.

proximo: (*Lat.*) next month.

psoas abscess: an abscess of the loin muscle, usually associated with tuberculosis.

public: an inn; an alehouse.

publican: 1: an innkeeper or tavern keeper. 2: a person who collects fees of any kind such as tithes, tolls, tribute, customs, etc.

puella: (*Lat.*) girl; sweetheart.

puer: (*Lat.*) boy; child; young man.

puerperal: related to childbirth.

puerperal exhaustion: the condition of which a woman died during childbirth (labor).

puerperal fever: childbed fever; septic poisoning which sometimes occurred during childbirth.

puerperium: a woman's confinement during and immediately after childbirth.

puffer: a person who attends auctions with the purpose of offering bids to run up the price.

puggard: a thief.

puking fever: milk sickness.

pulter: poultry.

Pulver Wednesday: Ash Wednesday.

puncheon: a large cask used for beer, wine, etc., with a liquid measure of varying capacity (72-120 gallons).

punky: a chimney sweeper.

pupil: a young person under the care of a guardian; in civil law, a boy or girl who has not yet reached the age of puberty (under 14 if male, and under 12 if female).

pupillus: (*Lat.*) orphan boy.

pur auter vie: (*Lat.*) time period; for the life of another.

purchased court: a court session which was not held on a regular court schedule, the costs paid for by the plaintiff and defendant.

purser: the officer in charge of provisions and who keeps the ship's accounts.

purser's name: a false name given by impressed seamen.

putila: (*Lat.*) little girl.

putillus: (*Lat.*) little boy.

putrid fever: a name for typhus fever or diphtheria.

Q

Quadragesima: a moveable feast day, Quadragesima Sunday, the sixth Sunday before Easter.

quadrimus: (*Lat.*) of four years, four years old.

quadroon: child of a mulatto and a white; a child with one black grandparent.

quae spondet infantis loco: (*Lat.*) godmother.

quee vide: (*Lat.*) [*abbrev.* q.v.] which see (plural).

quaire: a pamphlet or a book.

quarrier: a quarry worker.

quarryman: one who works in a quarry; a quarrier.

quartage: a tax, pension, or salary paid quarterly.

quarter: 1: a measure of grain which equals eight bushels or 1/4 ton. 2: in heraldry, any of the four equal divisions into which a shield is divided.

quartern: a fourth part of a standard weight; a loaf of bread weighing about four pounds.

Quarter Section: *see* Rectangular Survey System.

quarto: the page size of a book made up of sheets, each of which is folded into four leaves or eight pages.

que: (*Lat*) and.

quern: a small hand mill for grinding spices; a small mill for grinding grain.

questman: men, chosen annually, to assist church wardens in an inquiry and to present persons in need of punishment to the church court.

questmonger: one whose business is to conduct inquests.

quid pro quo: (*Lat.*) *literally* "value for value"; that which is received in consideration for something that is requested, done, or given.

quinine: a bitter, crystalline alkaloid, extracted from cinchona bark, used especially in the treatment of malaria.

Quinquagesima: a moveable feast day, Quinquagesima Sunday, the seventh Sunday before Easter.

quinsy: an inflammation of the tonsils accompanied by the formation of pus.

quire of paper: one-twentieth of a ream of paper; twenty-four or twenty-five sheets of paper equal in size and stock.

quit-claim deed: a deed releasing claim to an estate or property by an individual to another person.

quit-rent: a fee paid to a feudal lord so that the tenant could farm the land without being obligated to serve the lord in other capacities. *See* rent.

quit rent fee: in early Virginia, an annual fee (1 shilling for 50 acres of land) paid to the king in exchange for the right to live on and farm the property.

quod est: (*Lat.*) which is.

quod vide: (*Lat.*) which see.

quorum: the legal number of persons required to be present to conduct business.

R

rack rent: a very high excessive rent.

ragman's-roll: a register, compiled by a representative of the pope, of the benefices in Scotland.

rake: a man who is dissolute or debauched.

raker: 1: a person who raked the streets and removed the filth. 2: a scavenger.

rakeshame: (*obsolete*) a vile, dissolute wretch.

rambooze: [*also* rambuse] a drink made of wine, ale, eggs, and sugar in the wintertime and of wine, milk, sugar, and rose water in the summertime.

ram mutton: undesirable meat.

range: the area between range lines (north-south running lines) as a part of the Rectangular Survey System—together with the township lines (east-west running lines) range lines form areas of six miles square or 36 square miles, called townships.

range lines: the north-south running lines in the Rectangular Survey System laid off six miles apart east and west of the principle meridian. *See* Rectangular Survey System; range.

rape: a division of a county in Sussex, England; an intermediate division between a hundred and a shire, containing three or four hundreds.

raser: a dry measurement equaling four bushels.

raser house: a barber's shop.

ratoner: a rat catcher.

ratsbane: rat poison; trioxide of arsenic.

ratten: 1: to destroy or take away machinery, tools, etc. 2: to force an employer to bow to union demands.

ravener: one who plunders.

readings-out: the Society of Friends Church records kept of those members who were read-out-of-meeting, or dismissed.

real: an old Spanish coin of silver equal to a quarter of a peseta—eight reals made one dollar, hence "pieces of eight."

real property: land and anything permanently attached to it, Including buildings and growing timber, as well as the rights issued in ownership of the land.

realty: [*also* fast estate] land and tenements.

ream: 1: cream; the cream-like froth on ale. 2: an amount of paper from 480 sheets or 20 quires to 516 sheets or 21 1/2 quires a printer's ream.

reap hook: a sickle; a curved blade of steel with a short handle used for reaping or cutting a harvest.

receiver: a person who is appointed by the court to hold property while the settlement of a suit is pending.

receivership: guardianship.

recognitor: in English law, one of a jury on an assize.

recognizance: a promise made before a court or magistrate to do a certain thing such as appear before court, not leave a specific area, etc.

reconveyance: a deed in which property that has been sold to another person is transferred back to the original owner.

Rectangular Survey System: a method of surveying property provided for under the Land Ordinance of 1785 passed by the Continental Congress which divided the public land states into thirty-seven separate survey systems, each separate survey consisting of a starting point, an east-west running base line, and a north-south running principal meridian (P.M.).

redar: 1: one who interprets dreams. 2: a pocket-book.

redback: a certificate printed on red paper and issued by Texas in 1834, which became worthless when Texas was unable to pay interest on them.

redemption: the regaining of property once lost to forfeiture or foreclosure.

Redemptioners: early Pennsylvania Germans who, as indentured servants, paid for their passage from Europe.

redubbor: a person who bought stolen cloth and resold it after it had been dyed or otherwise disguised.

reeve: 1: a churchwarden; a minor parish official. 2: *see* reve.

reformado: an officer who has been removed from command but bears his rank and draws his pay.

Refugee Tract: a tract of land given to patriots in 1789 whose property had been confiscated by the British.

registrar: an official who registers/records events such as land transactions, probates, births, deaths, etc.

regnal years: the years as listed by reign of a king or queen. *See* anno regni.

regulator: a private citizen who banded with others to punish lawbreakers on the frontier (on the Pacific frontier of the 1850s such bands of private citizens were called vigilantes).

release of dower: *see* dower release.

relict: (*Lat.*) a widow or widower; the surviving spouse.

relicta: (*Lat.*) widow.

relictus: (*Lat.*) widower.

relinquishment land: land sold without title to its minerals, which remained vested in the state.

remainder: the part of the estate that is left after a prior interest ends.

remainderman: the person to whom the remainder of an estate is given.

Reminissnere: a moveable feast day, the second Sunday in Lent, the fifth before Easter.

remitter: in law, the restitution of a more ancient and certain right to a person who has right to land, but is out of possession.

remitting fever: malaria.

removal: in church records, the entry of a member removed from the church records in good standing.

rent: in common law, 1: rent-service is when some corporal service is incident to it, as by fealty and a sum of money. 2: rent-charge is when the owner of the rent has no future interest or reversion expectant in the land, but the rent is reserved in the deed without any clause of distress. 3: rents of assize [also quit-rent] are certain established rents of free-holders and copy-holders of manors which cannot be varied.

repeater: 1: one who votes more than once in an election. 2: a ship that accompanies an admiral in each fleet and whose duty was to carry messages to other ships in the fleet.

replevin: an action or lawsuit to recover a specific item which was either detained or taken from a person rather than asking for the value of the item taken.

Republican calendar: [also French Republican calendar] a calendar abolished by Napoleon in August 1805 in which the year was divided into 12 months, each of which was 30 days long and was subdivided into three 10-day periods known as decades, and the last day of each decade was set aside as a day of rest. The five days remaining at the end of the year (September 17 through 21 in the Gregorian calendar) were designated national holidays. Three months were assigned to each season.

requiescat in pace: (*Lat.*) may he or she rest in peace.

residuary bequest: a bequest which consists of anything left over after the fees and debts have been paid in an estate.

residuary clause: a clause in **a** will which conveys any and everything left of a residuary legacy to the beneficiary.

residuary devisee: beneficiary in a will who is to take all real property remaining after other legacies have been satisfied.

residuary estate: all the rest and residue; everything that has not been disposed of other than what remains in the residuary clause.

residue: the surplus of a testator's estate when all other obligations have been legally taken care of.

residuum: (*Lat.*) the remainder of an estate after all debts and legacies have been dispersed.

restraint on alienation: restriction placed on owners which makes it impossible to convey real property interests.

reticule: a small net-work handbag carried by women.

retting hemp: the process of preparing flax or hemp by getting it wet or exposing it to the dew so that the woody part would be softened and could be separated from the filament part.

reve: [*also* reeve] a bailiff of a manor.

revenuer: a federal officer whose duty it is to enforce laws against distilling untaxed liquor.

revenue stamp: a stamp placed on goods and documents to show that the tax had been collected.

reverse index: in probate, an index listing those involved in the probate process, not the deceased.

reversion: an estate that will return to the original owner after the expiration of a grant or when a certain condition has not been met; land returned to the government for lack of adherence to conditions relating to the use.

reversioner: one who has a reversion; one who has lands returned to him because of a clause in a will or transfer of land.

revestiary: dressing room in a church.

revocation: cancellation; annulment.

revulsion: in medicine, the act of diverting humors or any cause of disease from one part of the body to another.

rex: (*Lat.*) king; master; leader.

rheumatism: a painful disease affecting muscles and joints, chiefly the larger joints.

riband: in heraldry, an ordinary placed on the field of a shield, usually a band placed diagonally on the shield.

rickets: a disease of the skeletal system resulting from a deficiency of calcium or vitamin D in the diet, or from lack of sunlight.

riddle: a large sieve.

ride: a saddle horse.

riding: an administrative district, found mostly in England.

rigadoon: a lively, brisk dance for one couple, done with a quick jumping step, usually in double time.

rigger: one who worked with the rigging of a ship.

right: a document, issued to the county surveyor, which established a person's right to lands or allowed the surveyor to survey the land desired by the potential patentee.

rigor: a stiffness and rigidity of the body which does not respond to stimuli; shivering or trembling with a chill preceding a fever.

ringled: married.

riparian: a person who lives on the banks of a river.

ripper: a person who brings fish inland to the market.

rippier: see cashmarie—"there might be a distinction in that the rippier took his/her fish from the riverbank and the cashmarie took his/her fish from the sea coast."—*The Source.*

River Brethren: see Brethren church.

riverman: unlicenced employee of a river boat, such as agent, barker, bartender, clerk, cook, deck hand, and so on—usually does not refer to the owner, master, mate, or pilot (however, such is not always the case).

river workers: itinerant workers with varied occupations such as grist miller, blacksmith, entertainer, or trader, who took to river travel and plied their trade as they went.

road agent: 1: (*New England*) a surveyor. 2: (*esp. American West*) a highwayman on stagecoach routes.

roadster: a horse used for riding on the road; a bicycle; a person who travels or wanders.

roberdsmen: a class of lawless and marauding vagabonds in fourteenth-century England.

rod: a unit of land measure equal to a pole or perch (16.5 feet or 5.5 yards).

rodman: a surveyor's assistant who carries a leveling rod.

Rogation Week: in England, the week during which the parishioners observed the custom of perambulating (reaffirming or preserving) the land boundaries of those living in the parish.

rogue money: in England, money paid to the High Constable from each parish or hundred for the annual keep of prisoners.

rollster: roster.

romage: rummage

rood: 1: a unit of measure which equals one-quarter of an acre (40 square rods) 2: a length of 5.5 to 8 yards.

roper: a rope or net maker.

rope ripe: fit for hanging; deserving of a rope.

rope walk: a factory which makes rope; the long passage in a factory for laying strands to be made into rope.

rother: 1: the rudder of a ship. 2: a bovine animal.

rounder: 1: a Methodist circuit preacher. 2: a habitual criminal who made the rounds from workhouses to saloons to prison. 3: a boring-toot.

Roundhead: 1: a seventeenth-century member of the English Parliamentary Party. 2: a Puritan.

roundhouse: 1: a constables prison. 2: a place with a turning area in the center for the repair of railroad cars.

rout: a disorderly group of people; a large social gathering of fashionable people, usually an evening occasion; a huge defeat.

rover: an archer; a pirate ship.

rubeola: German measles.

rue bargain: a bad bargain; the forfeit paid for withdrawing from a bargain.

rumfustian: a drink made of a quart of strong beer, a bottle of wine or sherry, half a pint of gin, the yolk of twelve eggs, orange peel, nutmeg, spices, and sugar.

runaway: an indentured servant or slave who left without permission.

rundlet: [*also* runlet] a small cask measuring 18 gallons of liquid or 15 gallons in English measurement.

runner: 1: a smuggler; a smuggling ship. 2: a messenger, collector, or agent.

ruricola: (*Lat.*) husbandman.

rus: (*Lat.*) county; county seat; farm.

russel: woolen cloth of close-grained twill, very durable, and commonly used for women's and children's shoes.

Rueselite: a member of the Jehovah's Witnesses.

rustica: (*Lat.*) country girl.

rusticus: (*Lat.*) rural.

rustler: 1: a cattle thief. 2: a domestic animal that looks after itself under all conditions.

S

sacerdotalism: doctrine which teaches that salvation is aided by mediation of priests with God in behalf of men.

sacrament: in ancient Rome, a military oath taken by a Roman soldier not to desert his standard; a solemn oath or promise ratified by a formal rite.

sacrarium: a sanctuary in a Christian Church.

sad iron: fiat iron for pressing clothes.

safe conduct: a document allowing specified persons and/or goods to pass safely through military regions or other specified areas.

sail-fan: a particular kind of fan used in winnowing corn.

sail loft: a building or loft where sails are cut and made.

Saint Anthony's fire: *see* erysipelas.

Saint Elmo's fire: an electric charge which resembles a flame and can be seen at prominent points on a ship at sea.

Saint Hugh's bones: shoemaker's tools.

Saint Vitus's dance: chorea, especially of children.

salamander: various articles and implements which can withstand heat or are used in the fire; a person who can withstand great heat.

saleratus: a leavening agent; baking powder.

Salic Law: law introduced by the Salian Franks into France around the fifth century A.D.; one of the most famous of these laws was the practice of excluding women from inheriting landed estates and not allowing them to succeed to the crown.

saloonist: a saloon keeper; one who promoted the idea of having saloons for drinking.

salt fund: contributions of money for the poor and veterans' families.

salt peter: potassium nitrate; sodium nitrate. *See* niter.

salter: a maker of and dealer in salt; a drysalter.

saltern: a salt works; a place where salt is made by boiling or evaporation.

saltpeter house: a hospital for aged women in Paris; formerly, a prison for women.

Sambo: persons of various degrees of mixed black and Indian or European blood.

sampler: pieces of needlework suitable for framing and usually bearing an inspirational thought.

sandesman: a messenger; envoy; ambassador.

sand lotter: applied to the followers of Dennis Kearney, the leader of a socialist or communist party which existed from 1877 to 1880.

sandwichman: one who advertises by wearing two boards over his shoulders, one in front and one in back, with displays printed on them.

sanguinous crust: a scab.

sans issue: without issue.

sappers and miners: soldiers who belonged to the engineer corps whose duty was to make trenches or saps.

sarcoma: cancer.

sarsparilla: a carbonated drink flavored with the tropical plant of the genus Smilax.

sartor: a tailor.

sassafras: dried root bark of the sassafras tree, used in medicine and for flavoring.

sawyer: one who cuts timber into logs or boards.

saxifrage: a medicine that has the property of dissolving stones in the bladder.

Saxons: an ancient Germanic people who lived in northern Germany and conquered parts of England in the fifth and sixth centuries A.D.

sayer: a poet.

say weaver: a weaver of say, a cloth of fine texture resembling serge.

scaldhead: a scab infection of the head.

scale dish: a shallow bowl used for skimming milk.

scantling: a measuring rod used by a carpenter; a measurement; timber cut into small pieces to be used for studs, rails, etc.

scarlatina: "scarlet fever; commonly referred to as the canker rash."—*Webster's*

scarlet fever: a disease in which the body is covered with a red rash first appearing on the neck and breast, and accompanied by a sore throat.

scarlet rash: roseola.

schepel: a dry measurement equaling approximately three-fourths of a bushel.

schepen: a magistrate in the Dutch colonies.

schrimpschonger: one who carves bone, ivory, etc., into pieces of art.

sciatica: rheumatism in the hip.

scilicet: (*Lat.*) that is; to say; evidently; of course; no doubt.

scire facias: (*Lat.*) *literally* "you make known"; a writ based on records by which a person is required to show why the record should not be enforced.

scire feci: (*Lat.*) *literally* "I have made known"; the return issued by a sheriff to a writ of scire facias letting it be known the writ has been served.

scirrhus: a cancerous tumor on any part of the body, usually made up of fibrous connective tissue.

scold: a person, especially a woman, who habitually used abusive language against other persons.

scoop wagon: Conestoga wagon.

scooter: 1: a sailboat with a fiat bottom and runners used on water or ice. 2: a plow used for laying out furrows and breaking up soil.

scotomy: dizziness or nausea, with dimness of sight.

scout: 1: a spy. 2: an Oxford University servant or waiter. 3: a fast Dutch sailboat.

scribe: an official clerk or transcriber; one who copied manuscripts before printing was developed.

scrimer: a fencing master.

scrimshander: scrimshaw.

scrimshaw: decoration and carving of shells, bone, ivory, etc.

scrip: (*archaic*) a small wallet. 2: specially issued paper money.

script: handwriting; something written.

scrivener: a clerk or notary; formerly, a moneylender; a broker.

scrivener's palsy: writer's cramp.

scrofula: a disease, called the King's Evil, characterized by tumors in the glands of the neck; tuberculosis of lymph glands.

scrumpox: a pustular disease of the skin. *See* impetigo.

scrutineer: an examiner of votes at an election.

scudder: a swift runner.

scurvy: a disease characterized by great debility, a pale bloated face, and bleeding spongy gums, indicant to persons who live confined, or on salted meats without fresh vegetables.

scutage: a payment of money made in lieu of military service; a tax levied against a knight's fees and paid to the feudal lord to pay for men at arms.

scutch: 1: to dress by beating, such as separating individual fibers of cotton after they have been loosened and cleaned; an implement for dressing flax or hemp. 2: to cut into lengths.

scythe: a tool with a long curved blade and a sharp edge, fastened at an angle to a handle bent into a convenient form for swinging the blade.

Sea Fencibles: a group organized during the War of 1812 against Britain, which was the first organization of the U.S. Army charged exclusively with coastal defense and along with the Flotilla Service, of protecting ports, harbors, and the coast.

Sea Island cotton: a fine, long fibered cotton originally grown in the Sea Islands.

sea lawyer: 1: a shark. 2: a sailor, with slight knowledge, who likes to argue about points of sea law.

sealer: a person who inspects, tests, and certifies weights and measures.

searcher: one who is employed at a custom-house station to inspect incoming goods; one who inspects meat or goods in factories to ensure quality.

seat: to settle or form an area, such as to seat a county; a large house that is part of a country estate; the town where an important ruler makes his home.

seating and planting: as a part of the headright system, a patent (title) to land based on two conditions: the payment of one shilling per fifty acre quitrent fee, and that either a house be built and stock raised or one acre of ground be cultivated within three years.

secessionist: one who advocated the right of a state to withdraw from the Union.

second papers: [*also* final papers] the petition, oath of allegiance, naturalization certificate, or all three.

section: a measurement used in the Rectangular Survey System which equals 640 acres or one square mile.

security: a person who will vouch to be liable for a sum of money if a person fails to appear in court.

See: the rank or office of a bishop.

seedsman: one who deals in seeds; a sower.

seignior: a lord of a manor.

seigniorage: a duty levied on money coined to cover the expenses of minting; a royalty claimed on certain minerals that were mined.

seine: a drift net, one that is held up by corks and weighted at the bottom so it floats perpendicularly, for catching fish.

seisin: [*also* seizin] a freehold (held in fee or for life) estate—at one time land could only be held in seisin, because all land was owned by the reigning sovereign.

seized: to be the legal fee simple possessor.

seizin: *see* seisin.

selectman: in New England, one of three to seven men, chosen annually, to manage the affairs of a small town.

sempster: [*also* sempstress] a seamstress.

senex: (*Lat.*) old man; old woman; aged.

Senior: [*also* Sr.] the older of two persons having the same name, but who are not necessarily related. *See* Junior.

senium: (*Lat.*) old age.

sennachie: a Scottish tribal genealogist.

Separatists: [*also* Independents] those who withdrew from the Church of England in the sixteenth century.

Sephardim: Spanish or Portuguese Jews.

sept: a branch of a Scottish highland clan.

septicemia: blood poisoning.

Septuagesima: a moveable feast day, Septuagesima Sunday, the ninth Sunday before Easter.

sepulchered: [*also* sepultured] buried.

sepulcralis: (*Lat.*) funeral.

sepulcrum: (*Lat.*) grave.

sepultered: *see* sepulchered.

sequela: one who follows; in medicine, a diseased condition resulting from a previous sickness.

sequentia: (*Lat.*) the following.

sequester: to renounce a claim to an inheritance; to place goods or property with a third person until a settlement can be made; to take or seize property of someone until the profits of the property are paid.

serf: a slave; one who was bound with a master's land and was sold with the land when it changed hands.

sergeanty: a type of service performed for the kings in exchange for a feudal tenure.

serva: (*Lat.*) maid servant.

servery: a butler's pantry; a room from which meals are served.

servula: (*Lat.*) servant girl.

servus: (*Lat.*) servant; slave.

set over: refers to the process or releasing custody of an indentured servant to the highest bidder.

settlor: a grantor of property, a trustor.

Seven-br: [*also* 7br] in the Old Style calendar, September.

Seven Ranges: first land surveyed under the rectangular survey system by the government west of the Ohio River and part of the Ohio Land Grant, 1786.

severalty: property held by one person only and not jointly or in common.

sewing clerk: a district collector of sewing done by glove makers who worked in the home.

sewster: a seamstress.

sexagenarian: a person between 60 and 70 years of age.

Sexagesima: a moveable feast day, Sexagesima Sunday, the eighth Sunday before Easter, the second Sunday before Lent.

sexennial: a happening which occurs every six years.

sextary: "an old Roman liquid measure containing the sixth part of a congius; a dry measure containing the sixteenth part of a modius."—Oxford

shades: *see* silhouette.

shadowgraph: *see* silhouette.

shakefork: 1: a pitchfork. 2: in heraldry, a bearing which is Y-shaped and has bluntly pointed ends.

shakes: "a convulsive trembling, often accompanying intermittent fever, alcoholism, etc."—*Webster's*

shaking: the ague; a chill.

shalloons: woolen material used for lining coats.

shallop: a dinghy fitted with oars or sails and sometimes both.

shambles: (*colonial New England*) a slaughterhouse, or place where meat was butchered and sold.

shandygaff: a mixture of ale and ginger beer, or of lager beer and ginger ale, etc.

shanghai: sailors kidnapped for crew duty.

shank's mare: one's feet—to ride on shank's mare means to walk.

shanty: a hut; *(Australia)* a public house.

shanty boat: a small, flat-decked boat with a cabin used by lumbermen as their homes.

shanty-man: a lumberman.

sharecropper: a person who would farm ground owned by another, and divide the crops or the profits with the owner.

shave: to buy a promissory note by paying the owner less than the value.

shaving horse: a bench or trestle mostly used in tanning leather.

shearman: one who shears cloth, metal, etc.

sheepbiter: a petty thief.

sheepman: a person whose business is raising sheep; a sheepherder.

sheepshead: 1: a sheep's head prepared as food. 2: a foolish person.

sheepskin: 1: parchment prepared from the leather. 2: a diploma.

shellback: a hardened or experienced sailor.

shepster: a female pattern cutter; a dressmaker.

sheriff's deed: a deed created by the sheriff at the sale of land confiscated for failure to pay taxes.

shift: a change of clothing. *See* chemise.

shift-marriage: crossroads wedding.

shill: 1: a combined hearse and mourning coach. 2: a decoy or fraud.

shilling: an English coin equaling twelve pennies or one twentieth of a pound.

shingles: [*also* herpes zoster] an acute virus disease marked by small blisters on the skin along the course of a nerve.

shinny: a simple form of hockey, played with a ball and sticks, popular with children.

ship fever: a form of typhus fever.

ship husband: one employed by the owners of a ship to oversee repairs, etc., while the ship is in harbor.

ship master: the owner or commander of a ship.

shipwright: a person who constructs or repairs ships.

shire: a county in Great Britain.

shirereeve: a bailiff or steward of a manor.

shoddy: inferior woolen yarn or cloth made from reprocessed fibers.

shoe-finder: a person who sells shoemakers' tools and appliances.

shoe-pack: a shoe of tanned leather that does not have a separate sole, somewhat like a moccasin.

shoe stone: a whetstone used by a shoemaker.

shoe-wiper: a servant whose duty it is to clean shoes.

shop walker: 1: a floorwalker in a department store. 2: an assistant exercising general supervision over a department of a ship.

shoresman: a person who makes his living on the shore in the fishery business; a shore-gunner.

shot tower: a high tower from which molten lead is dropped in a liquid, thus forming hard globules or shot.

shoulder-clapper: a bailiff.

shrieve: a sheriff.

shroud: a cloth used in wrapping a corpse for burial.

Shrovetide: the three days before Ash Wednesday; a period of time set aside for confession and festivity just before Lent.

sibman: kinsman.

sic: (*Lat.*) *literally* "thus"—used to show that a quoted passage, often containing some error, is precisely reproduced.

side board: a piece of dining room furniture with drawers or shelves, used to hold linen, silver, china, etc.

sidemen: a churchwarden's assistant; a party man.

signator: (*Lat.*) signer; witness.

signum: a mark made in place of a signature.

silhouette: [*also* shade; shadowgraph] profiles of a person cut from black silk or paper and mounted in a frame or album.

silk throwster: a person who winds, twists, spins, or throws silk fibers in preparation for weaving.

silver rent: rent that is paid in money rather than kind or goods.

similiter: a pleading wherein the second party agrees to a trial by jury.

sinapism: a plaster composed of mustard seed pulverized with some other ingredients and used as an external application.

sine: (*Lat.*) without.

sin eater: a person who was hired at funerals to take the sins of the deceased upon oneself.

sine die: (*Lat.*) *literally* "without a day"; dismissing a proceeding, such as a court term, without determining a day for it to begin again.

sine loco: (*Lat.*) without place.

sine prole: (*Lat.*) without issue; without children.

sine prole supersite: (*Lat.*) without surviving issue (children).

single tree: [*also* swingle tree; whiffletree] a form of swingle tree, the horizontal crossbar to which the traces of a harnessed horse are fastened;

sirasis: an inflammation of the brain, caused by excessive heat of the sun; frenzy peculiar to children.

sister-bairn: the child of a sister; the child of an aunt.

sitio: a league, 4,428.4 acres, or 13,889 square feet.

sitting: a seat in a church paid for in the form of rent.

skepe: a wooden pan used when separating wheat from chaff.

skiff: a long narrow rowboat, sometimes equipped with a sail.

skinker: a tapster; one who draws ale.

skinner: one who deals in animal skins; a mule driver.

Skinners: a roving band of adventurers active during the American Revolution who stole from either side and remained neutral.

skip kennel: a lackey; a footboy or footman.

skippie: a measure of three pecks.

skirret: the water parsnip.

slasher: a machine used for sizing warp yarns.

slater: one who slates roofs.

slay: [*also* sley] a weaver's tool, one of the guideways of a knitting machine.

slinger: one who used a sling in ancient warfare.

slippery elm: the inner bark of a North American elm used as medication.

slitting mill: a mill where nails are made by slitting iron bars.

sloes: milk sickness.

sloop: a small sailing vessel with one mast.

slop: (*naval slang*) the clothes and bedding of a sailor; an outer garment made of linen such as a nightgown, cloak, or mantle.

Slop Book: in the British Navy, a register of personal supplies given to the men such as clothing, soap, tobacco, and religious books.

slop seller: a person who sold cheap, ready-made garments.

slop shop: a shop where cheap, ready-made clothes are sold.

slumgullion: 1: the refuse which drains from a whale while being cut up. 2: a drink of weak tea or coffee. 3: a meat and vegetable stew.

small clothes: eighteenth-century knee breaches.

small means: little money.

small pox: a very contagious disease characterized by fever and eruptions on the skin.

smelter: 1: one who works in a smelter melting down ores. 2: a fisherman who fishes for smelts.

smiddy: a smithy.

smith: one who makes or repairs metal items.

smithy: the shop of a smith.

smock mill: a type of windmill in which only the top part was turned to face the wind.

smoke jack: the device used for turning meat on a spit in the fireplace, moved by currents of air rising up the chimney.

smoker's patch: a smooth, white patch on the tongue due to excessive smoking.

snake fence: an interlocking rail fence made in a zigzag pattern.

snakeroot: any of a variety of plants supposedly good for snakebite, the most widely known being the Virginia snakeroot.

snakestone: see madstone.

snipe: any of several game birds with slender bills.

snob: 1: in certain English universities, a townsman as op-

posed to a gownsman. 2: persons who work for lower wages during a strike. 3: a shoemaker or cobbler.

snobber: a shoemaker or cobbler.

snow warden: a person whose duty was to make sure the snow was evenly dispersed on the streets so the sleigh runners could move easily.

soapboiler: a soap-maker.

soapstone: a soft stone having a soapy feel and composed of talc, chlorite, and often magnetite used to clean griddles, bedwarmers, etc.

sobrina: (Lat.) [also sobrinus] first cousin; cousin-german.

socage: a system of land tenure by which a tenant could live on and work the land in return for services given to a lord that were not military in nature—when the service was an honorable one it was called free socage and when it was considered base it was called villein socage.

socer: [also socerus] father-in-law.

soceri: (*Lat.*) parents-in-law.

socerus: *see* socer.

sock: 1: a ploughshare. 2: the drainage of a dunghill (liquid manure).

sock and scythe: ploughing and mowing.

socrus: (*Lat.*) mother-in-law.

softening of the brain: apoplexy.

solicitor: a local court appointed official; *(Britain) a* lawyer who can only practice in lower courts due to a lack of bar membership.

sooner: a person who tried to occupy public land before it was legal to do so.

sop: bread soaked in milk, water, or juices from food.

soporose: [*also* soporous] causing sleep; affected with coma.

soror: (*Lat.*) sister; female companion or friend.

sorois: (*Lat.*) sister.

soukinge free: foster brother.

soul silver: a fee paid to a church or parish on behalf of a deceased person.

souse: a pickled food, especially the feet, ears, and head of pig.

souter: a shoemaker; a cobbler.

Southwest Territory: the region established in 1790, officially known as the Territory of the U.S. South of the Ohio River.

spallier: a tin works laborer.

spalling hammer: an ax-shaped hammer used by a mason in rough-dressing stones.

Spanish Influenza: pandemic influenza.

Spanish real: a silver coin worth one-eighth of a dollar. *See* eleven-penny bit.

sparable: a small nail, without a head, used by shoemakers.

specie: minted coins made of metal.

speculator: one who bought and sold land, or blacks during slavery times.

spermaceti: a white, waxy substance obtained from whale oil used to make candles and oint-ments.

sperviter: a keeper of sparrow hawks

sphragistics: the science of engraved seals or signets.

spicer: a grocer or one who deals in spices.

spider: a fry pan with long at-tached legs used to cook over an open fire.

spina bifida: a deformity of the base of the spine.

spinner: one who spins yarn.

spinster: *literally* a woman who spins; more often, an unmarried woman or a woman who lives alone, such as a widow.

spital: 1: a hospital for the very poor and those having leprosy or other loathsome diseases. 2: a shelter for travelers on a road.

spite fence: a high or unsightly fence built primarily to spite a neighbor by hurting the value of his property.

spittle: a hospital.

spokeshave: a drawing-knife with a blade or plane-bit set be-tween two handles and used for planing curved work.

spoliation: 1: a writ or suit brought by one incumbent against another holding the same benefice by an illegal or questionable title. 2: the action of destroying a document, or tampering with it in such a way evidence.

sponsor: bondsman.

sponsus: (*Lat.*) betrothed; bride-groom; suitor.

spotted fever: cerebrospinal meningitis fever, characterized by inflammation of the cere-brospinal meninges; typhus.

spotter: a detective hired to look for dishonest employees.

sprue: a chronic tropical dis-ease characterized by anemia, gastrointestinal disorders, sore throat, etc.

spurius: (*Lat.*) illegitimate; bas-tard.

spurrier: a person who made spurs.

squatter: a person who settles on public land or the property of another person without any claim or title, and who cannot gain title to land no matter how long he has occupied the land.

squire: 1: a young man of high or noble birth who served as an attendant to a knight. 2: a title of respect given to a justice of the peace or local dignitary.

squirrel hunter: volunteer soldiers using squirrel guns who responded to a call for help to defend Cincinnati, Ohio in 1862.

Sr.: *see* Senior.

stake: 1: a small anvil used by blacksmiths and sheet-metal workers. 2: a church unit in the Church of Jesus Christ of Latter-day Saints composed of wards and sometimes a few branches.

stall: a pew or enclosed seat in the main part of a church; a seat near the stage in a theater separated by railing.

stallage: the right to and the rent paid for the erection of a stall at fairs.

stallman: one who keeps a stall at a market or fair; a man who works a stall he contracted for in a coal mine.

stall-wage: the payment given to a vicar by the canon whose parish he took charge of during his term of residence.

stamp: a machine used in leather manufacturing that softens the hides by pounding them in a vat.

stampman: a person who works with an ore-crushing stamp mill.

stamp mill: a machine consisting of pestles powered by water or steam used in crushing ore.

standard keeper: a public official who kept the standard set of weights and measures by which all other weights and measures were compared and must conformed to.

Stannotype: *see* tintype.

St. Anthony's fire: *see* Saint Anthony's fire.

stapler: a dealer in various goods.

Star-chamber: a court of criminal jurisdiction in England, abolished by Charles I.

state: to deed land to a person; to survey and build a road between two points.

State of Franklin: a state in existence from 1784 to February 1788 in the western lands of North Carolina (now a part of eastern Tennessee).

statesman: a small landholder.

stationer: a bookseller; one who sells paper, quills, ink stands, pencils, and other writing items.

status plat: a copy of a plat or survey containing the necessary information to determine federal ownership of public lands and resources.

statutory law: laws enacted by legislatures which take precedence over common law.

Strangite: *see* Cutlerite.

steam packet: a steam-powered ship.

steelyard: [*also* lever scale] a balance or weighing machine.

steeple house: a church.

steer: 1: (*obsolete*) a steersman or helmsman. 2: castrated male beef cattle.

steerage: a section in a passenger ship for those paying the lowest fare.

steersman: the helmsman of a ship.

St. Elmo's fire: *see* Saint Elmo's fire.

stemma: (*Lat.*) [*also* stemma gentile] pedigree.

stevedore: a workman employed either as overseer or laborer in loading and unloading the cargoes of merchant vessels.

steward: a person entrusted with the care and management of another's estate or household.

St. Hugh's bones: *see* Saint Hugh's bones.

still room: a room near the pantry where wines and preserves are kept.

stirpes: (*Lat.*) 1: a family or branch of family. 2: in law, the person from whom everyone in a family is descended.

stitcher: one who sews, decorates with stitching, etc.

stive: 1: a stew. 2: a kind of bagpipe. 3: to compress and stow gear in a ship's hold.

stiver: 1: a Dutch coin equal to 1/20 of a guilder, 2: (*obsolete*) a harlot.

stockinger: one who knits, weaves, or deals in stockings.

stoker: one who feeds or tends a furnace or fire, such as one employed to tend the fires on a steam engine.

stomacher: an ornamental girdle.

stomatitis: inflammation of the mucous membrane of the mouth.

stone cutter: one who cuts and dresses stones; a machine for trimming stones.

stone horse: stallion.

stoner: a person who cuts stones; a device used to remove stones from fruit.

stone rake: a sturdy hook-toothed rake used by farmers to collect stones used in the construction of road beds.

stranger's fever: yellow fever.

strangury: in medicine, a difficult and painful discharge of urine.

straw man: 1: a scarecrow. 2: a person used by another to disguise his true intentions, especially in politics.

street cleaner: a sweeper; a mudlark.

strong: 1: among teamsters, a whip. 2: a line of fencing.

struma: goiter or scrofula.

St. Vitus's dance: *see* Saint Vitus's dance.

subnuba: (*Lat.*) second wife; intruder; rival.

suborn: to induce someone through bribery or illegal methods to do something.

substitute broker: a person who took another's place in military service for a fee.

sucken: [*also* thirl] dues paid at a mill.

sudor anglicus: sweating sickness.

Sufferer: a Connecticut citizen who suffered at the hands of the

British and lost his/her home and was given a certificate for land in the Western Reserve.

suffrage: 1: a short prayer of supplication. 2: the right to vote.

sugar house: a small house or shack where maple sap is boiled down into sugar or syrup.

sugaring off: the cooling process of making sugar during which the product granulates and turns to sugar.

sui generis: (*Lat.*) of his own kind or race; individual; unique.

sui juris: (*Lat.*) *literally* "of his own right"; capable of making a contract and no longer dependant on another.

suit broker: a marriage broker, or one who made a business of obtaining the suits of petitioners at court.

suitor: a plaintiff in a law case.

sull: a plow.

Summary Court-Martial: a military or naval court, presided over by one commissioned officer, to try cases involving military personnel in service related

actions which has limited jurisdiction and authority, and all decisions may be appealed to a higher court.

summer complaint: diarrhea occurring in the summertime.

sumpter: a packhorse or mule; a porter.

sumptuary law: a law made to regulate morals, religion, or personal habits.

supercargo: an officer on a merchant ship who supervised the sales and commercial concerns of the voyage.

supersedeas: (*Lat.*) *literally* "you shall desist"; an order commanding a stay in proceedings.

supra: (*Lat.*) before; above.

supra scriprum: (*Lat.*) as written above.

surety: a guarantee or a person who assumes the responsibility for another such as one who promises to pay someone else's debts if he defaults.

surrender: a land record which involves giving up land before the lease has expired with the mutual consent of both parties.

surveyor's measure: a length of chain (a gunter's chain) measuring sixty-six feet.

susceptor: (*Lat.*) undertaker; receiver; godfather.

sutler: a person who followed an army camp peddling provisions and supplies.

suus: (*Lat.*) her own, its own, their own.

swage: a tool used for bending or shaping metal; a stamp used to shape or mark metal by hammering.

swailer: [*also* swaler; swealer] a miller or dealer in corn.

swain: 1: a herdsman; a servant; a young man who was a knight's attendant. 2: a lover.

swaler: *see* swailer.

swamper: 1: a laborer who clears roads in a swamp or forest. 2: a person who does odd jobs in a saloon.

swealer: *see* swailer.

sweating sickness: an acute, infectious, rapidly fatal disease epidemic in England in the fifteenth and sixteenth centuries.

sweetmeat: 1: any sweet food or delicacy prepared with sugar or honey. 2: a varnish used on patent leather.

swingle tree: *see* single tree.

switchel: a beverage of molasses and water with ginger, vinegar, or rum; any strong, sweetened beverage.

sword cutler: one who makes and mounts swords.

sword player: a fencer; a gladiator.

sworn brothers: brothers or companions in arms who, according to the laws of chivalry, vowed to share danger or success; close companions or associates.

syllabub: a mixture of wine, ale, or cider, with milk or cream to form a soft curd which was flavored with lemon juice or rose water.

syncope: in medicine, a fainting or loss of consciousness caused by a temporary deficiency of blood to the brain.

syphilitica: pertaining to the disease syphilis.

T

tabby: a plain soft silk or watered silk.

tabes: slow progressive emaciation of the body or its parts.

tabler: one who boards others or is a boarder himself.

taille: 1: a feudal tax imposed by a king or a lord. 2: a waist or bodice of a gown.

tailleur: 1: the dealer or banker in various French card games. 2: a person who made men's and sometimes women's outer garments, such as riding habits.

tabularium: (*Lat.*) archives; register office.

tack: tenure or tenancy of land or a benefice; the period of tenure; a customary payment levied by a feudal superior or corporation.

tacky: (*American South*) a poor white.

taedium vitae: (*Lat.*) weariness of life.

taffety: a thin linen or silk that was heavier than the taffeta of today.

tail: an estate which does not descend to heirs generally, but to the heirs of the donee's body in a direct line if the posterity continues in regular order and upon the death of the first owner without issue the estate is terminated.

Talbotype: a photographic process developed by William Henry Fox Talbot in 1839. *See* calotype.

talesman: a person who is chosen from the spectators in a court to fill out a jury to the required number of persons should someone fail to appear.

tallage: an arbitrary tax levied by Norman and early Angevin kings upon the towns and demesne lands of the Crown, hence, a tax levied upon feudal dependants by their superiors.

tallager: a person who assessed or collected tallage; a tax collector.

tallow chandler: a person who makes and sells tallow candles.

tally: originally, a stick with notches representing the amount of a debt owed or paid which was split lengthwise with the creditor and the debtor each taking half.

tally-clark: a person who counts votes; one who keeps track of cargo or merchandise.

tally ho: a coach pulled by four horses.

tally-husband: a man who cohabits without benefit of marriage.

tallyman: a person who sells goods on credit and is paid by installments.

tammy: a woolen material glazed to resemble alpaca.

tanglefoot: an intoxicating beverage, especially whisky.

tanist: 1: a governor of a country. 2: (*Ireland*) the heir apparent of a prince.

tankard bearer: a person employed in drawing and carrying water from public pumps and conduits.

tanner: one who tans or converts hides into leather.

tansy: 1: a bitter and aromatic plant, used in cooking, and medicinally to reduce fever. 2: a dish of the seventeenth century made of eggs, cream, rose water, sugar, and the juice of herbs such as endive, spinach, sorrel, or tansy.

tap house: a tavern or inn.

tapiser: one who makes tapestry; an upholsterer.

tapper: a tavern-keeper.

tapster: a barmaid or bartender.

tartar emetic: a poisonous, white, crystalline salt used to increase perspiration and cause coughing, spitting, and vomiting.

task: originally, a tax; a fixed payment to a king, lord, or feudal superior.

tasker: a reaper or thresher.

task work: piecework; forced labor.

tawer: one who makes white leather.

teamer: a teamster.

teamster: one who drives a team for hauling cargo.

tectum: (*Lat.*) house; abode; dwelling.

tempore: (*Lat.*) in the time of.

tempus: (*Lat.*) time; season; occasion.

tempus fugit: (*Lat.*) as time passes (flies).

temse: a sieve or strainer used in brewing.

temse bread: bread made of finely sifted flour.

temulentus: (*Lat.*) intoxicated.

tenancy: residence on, and use of land, without owning it.

tenancy at will: tenancy which continues so long as the landlord or the tenant wish to continue it and which may be terminated "at the will" of the landlord or the tenant upon notice.

tenancy by the entirety: the ownership of property by a husband and wife together in which on the death of one the entire interest in the property diverts to the other—property that is owned by both the husband and the wife will pass to the survivor no matter what the will states.

tenancy in common: property that is held by two persons—in tenancy in common the right of survivorship does not apply. In this case the property automatically becomes part of the estate and is taken care of according to the terms of the will.

tenant: a name used for indentured servants who were settled on farms, supplied with tools, and engaged to remain on the land seven years; one who holds property by ownership or temporarily by leasing or renting.

tenant farmer: a renter or one who is allowed to farm a particular piece of land in trade for services given; farmer who did not own the land worked.

tenants-in-capite: a person holding feudal land directly from the king, usually several manors, who would in turn sub-infeud to other tenants.

tenant in common: a possession of the land as a whole by several persons, each having a separate title, although the land is not divided.

ten-ber: [*also* 10ber] in the Old Style calendar, December.

tenement: any property that can be held, but most often refers to houses and land.

tenne: in heraldry, a seldom used tawny (chestnut brown) color sometimes called stains.

tenor: the exact wording in a legal document or an exact copy.

tenter: one who looks after machinery in a factory, such as a loom tenter.

tenure: the right to hold and use property and rents accrued from property for an established period of time.

terce: a life-rent given by law to a widow, which consists of a third of her husbands estate on the condition that the marriage has lasted one year and a day, or that there is a living child of the marriage.

terce land: the rent from land given to a widow as her terce.

termer: a person who came to town when courts were in session, especially those who came for a dishonest purpose.

terminer: in law, a determining or an ending.

terrier: book or scroll used to record land description, usage, etc.

tertia: a division of infantry.

tertius: a third person; third generation.

testable: something that can be given by will; capable of making or witnessing a will.

testamentary: referring to, given by, or appointed by a will.

testamentary bond: security posted with the court by the executor of an estate to insure that the wishes of the deceased be followed.

testamentary guardian: a guardian appointed to be responsible for the inheritance of a minor child.

testamentum: (*Lat.*) will; testament.

testate: having a valid will upon death.

testator: the person who makes a will.

testatrix: a female who leaves a valid will.

teste: the concluding and witnessing clause of a writ or other legal document which expresses the date of its issue and the name of the judge.

testis: (*Lat.*) a witness.

tetanus: an infectious disease which attacks the muscles of the neck and lower jaw, caused by the tetanus bacillus, a germ which ordinarily infests the intestines of cattle or horses.

tetter: any of various skin diseases, such as eczema and impetigo.

tew: to soften, beat, or rend pliable when working with a fiber such as hemp.

thacker: a thatcher.

thatching-spale: a tool used by a thatcher with a forked blade and a cross handle at one end for thrusting tufts of straw.

thaumaturgy: performing magic or miracles.

thede: a people, race, or nation; a district occupied by a people.

theft-bote: the act of stealing.

Thermidor: in the Republican calendar, the month of heat.

Third Class city: a city in Kansas of the same order as an incorporated village in most states.

thirl: *see* sucken.

thoft fellow: a rower's bench.

thorn: (*Old English; Old Norse*) the runic character corresponding to the "th" sound of English.

thrombosis: a clot formation inside a blood vessel.

thrope: a village or small town.

throwster: one who throws (winds or twists) silk into thread.

thrush: a disease, usually contracted by children, caused by a fungus and characterized by milky-white lesions on the membranes of the mouth, lips, and throat; a disease contracted by horses which causes pus to form on the horse's foot.

tibican: (*Lat.*) flute player; piper.

tide mill: 1: a mill which gets its power from tidewater. 2: a mill used for clearing lands from tide-water.

tide waiter: a custom house officer.

tiller: a farmer; a cultivator.

tillman: a farmer; a ploughman.

timber claim: claim to land that was similar to homesteading but had specific requirements for planting and growing trees.

timwhiskey: [*also* gig; whiskey] a light, one-horse carriage with no top.

tincture: 1: a substance with medicinal properties, usually in an alcoholic solvent. 2: in heraldry, a name used to indicate any color, metal, or fur.

tinker: an itinerant repairman who mended pots and pans; a jack-of-all trades.

tinner: a worker in a tin mine; a tinsmith; one who makes tinware.

tinter: an artist skilled in tinting.

tintype: [*also* stannotype; ferrotype] a positive photograph taken directly on a piece of enameled tin plate, in which the picture was usually reversed.

tip: cart: *see* tumbrel.

tippling house: a tavern.

tipstaff: a bailiff or constable who carried a staff with a metal tip as an emblem of his office.

tire: a headdress worn by a woman, such as a hair ornament or a scarf.

tirewoman: a woman who assisted in the dressing room, especially in the theater; a dressmaker; a costumier.

tissue ballot: [*also* kiss-verse] ballots made from thin tissue paper which were hard to separate.

tithable: items upon which a fee may be levied such as farm animals, land, servants, etc.

tithe: associated with the payment of offerings (in kind or money) to a church or the government as a tax.

toiler: a tax collector.

tomus: (*Lat.*) volume; tome; one volume of a larger work.

tensor: (*Lat.*) barber.

tontine: an annuity subscribed to by several persons by which they all receive an annual amount from the funds—each time a member of the group dies the others receive an additional amount of money.

topmen: a sailor who serves in the top mast station; the man who stands at the topmost point when sawing lumber.

top sawyer: the man who took the upper stand in a saw pit.

topsman: the foreman or head cattle drover.

tort: a civil wrong other than a wrong involving contracts.

Tory: those living in America who refused to take an American oath of allegiance and sympathized with the British during the American Revolution—unlike the Loyalists, although the terms are used interchangeably, they would not wear British uniforms, were not as a general rule charged with treason, did not have their property seized, and were free to move from one place to another.

tote-road: a pack-road; roads made by horses carrying packs and heavy loads.

tow cloth: a coarse, heavy linen used during the eighteenth century for making serviceable clothes for slaves.

trace: a path made by the passage of animals, persons, and vehicles.

trammel: 1: a shackle for a horse that teaches it to amble. 2: a braid of hair. 3: a device used for drawing ellipses.

tramper: 1: a vagabond; a tramp. 2: a person who tramples or walks on clothing in the wash to clean them.

trampler: an attorney.

tranter: a peddler with a horse and cart.

traunt: to peddle or hawk (sell or pawn) goods.

traunter: a peddler.

traverse jury: a jury called to make judgments on an appeal from another jury.

tread road: a thoroughfare or roadway.

trebuchet: 1: *see* cucking stool. 2: a medieval war catapult used for hurling large stones. 3: a kind of balance or scale used for weighing coins. 4: a trap used for small game.

trembles: a disease of cattle and sheep caused by eating any of various poisonous weeds and characterized by muscular tremors and a stumbling gait.

trencherman: 1: a cook. 2: one who eats heartily. 3: a dependant or hanger-on.

trial jury: *see* petit jury.

trimmer: 1: one who has served prison time. 2: one who trims a ship by redistributing the cargo. 3: a shrewish person or a person who changes his opinions to suit the circumstances.

trine immersion: baptism by being immersed three times as practiced by the German Baptist Brethren Church who were often referred to as the Dunkers.

Trinitatis: a moveable feast day, Trinity Sunday, the eighth Sunday after Easter.

tritavus: (*Lat.*) great-grandfather's great-grandfather.

tronage: a toll or duty paid for weighing wool.

trover: 1: in law, the gaining possession of any goods, whether by finding or by other means. 2: smuggling, boot-legging, rum-running, poaching, salvage, and retrieval.

truchman: an interpreter.

truck system: paying in goods instead of money for services rendered.

trug: 1: a measure for wheat equal to two thirds of a bushel. 2: a shallow wooden pan for holding milk or a shallow wooden basket for carrying fruit and vegetables. 3: a prostitute.

trugging house: a house of prostitution.

trundle bed: a low bed on casters that can be pushed under a higher bed when not in use.

tubman: an English barrister in the Exchequer division of the High Court.

tucker: 1: a small cape or covering worn by a woman with a low-cut evening gown. 2: a fuller of cloth.

tumbrel: 1: *see* cuckingstool. 2: [*also* tip cart] a two-wheeled cart, used by farmers and for military purposes which was also used in the French Revolution to carry the condemned to the guillotine.

tumulo: (*Lat.*) to bury; to inter; to entomb.

tumulus: (*Lat.*) mound; grave; monument.

Tunkers: *see* Brethren church.

tunnel: a chimney flue.

turbary: in law, the right of a manorial villein or a copyholder to cut turf or fuel on the lord's property.

turf and twig: an ancient ceremony which involves the handing over of a clod of earth with a twig inserted symbolizing transfer of land.

turner: 1: a gymnast or a tumbler. 2: a person who works with a lathe.

tussis convulsiva: *see* whooping cough.

twibill: [*also* twilbil] a double-headed ax.

typhus: an acute infectious fever, characterized by high fever, dizziness, and headache.

U

unofficious will: a will made without any regard as to natural obligations of inheritance.

ulceration: loss of the surface covering, such as of skin or the mucous lining, of the intestine.

ulter: (*Lat.*) placed at a greater distance.

ultimo: (*Lat.*) in the month immediately preceding.

ultimo die: (*Lat.*) final day.

ultimus: (*Lat.*) last, end, furthest.

underground railroad: the system which took slaves to freedom in fourteen Northern states by 1830, and about 50,000 between 1840 and 1860.

unigena: (*Lat.*) only-begotten; only; of one family.

unigenitus: (*Lat.*) the only son.

union: a registration district in England made of two or more parishes (poor-law union).

unlaw: any transgression of the law, act of injustice, a fine, or a law that has no real authority.

unprobated will: a will which was never submitted for probate, which may have been lost for a time, etc.

unregistered will: will that has been proved but not entered into a volume of copy or registered wills at the probate court, either because an executor was not disposed to pay fees for registering, or because the probate court did not maintain registered copies at that period of time.

unseated: persons who were taxed for land that they owned but did not live on.

unseated land: unsettled area.

unsolemn will: a will where no executor is named.

urb: (*Lat.*) a walled town; city; citizen.

usher: in Great Britain, an assistant teacher.

usufruct: the right to enjoy property and the benefits thereof as long as the property itself is not harmed nor depleted.

userer: a money-lender, sometimes one who charged an especially high rate of interest.

usury: the practice of lending money at a rate of interest that is excessive or unlawfully high.

ut: (*Lat.*) in what manner, in the manner that.

uterine: having the same mother but different fathers.

ut infra: (*Lat.*) as below.

ut supra: (*Lat.*) as above.

uxor: (*Lat.*) wife; spouse; consort.

V

vacancy: 1: an opening referring to land or housing. 2: a pause or break in the workings of a probate court because of the death or resignation of the main official. 3: in Texas, an area of unsurveyed school land, not listed in land office records, between two or more recorded surveys.

vacant land: unappropriated public land, including land that has been occupied but on which no binding title had been given and the land thus reverted to the state.

vadlet: a servant, serving-man.

vail: a tip or bonus given to servants for work well done.

valid: that which is legally binding, legitimate, or good.

Vanity Book: a county (any local) history book for which people subscribed before the book was written on the condition their families would be included in its pages.

vara: an official measurement of land in Texas which equals 33 1/ 3 inches; 36 varas is 100 feet, 1900.8 varas is a mile, 5,645.4 square varas is one acre.

varioloid: a mild form of variola (smallpox) occurring in a person who has had a previous attack or who has been vaccinated.

varlet: 1: a youth acting as an attendant or serving as a knight's page. 2: a scoundrel; a rascal.

varletness: a girl or woman varlet.

varletry: the rabble; the mob.

vassal: in the Middle Ages, a person who held land under the feudal system by pledging loyalty to a lord and performing services, military or otherwise, in return for his protection.

vault: a latrine.

vel: (*Lat.*) or; even, even as; at least.

Vendemiaire: in the Republican calendar, the month of vintage.

venditioni exponas: a writ

venditioni exponas: a writ commanding an officer to put up for sale goods which were taken by the court in execution of a will.

vendue: a public auction or sale.

venesection: the opening of a vein for letting blood; phlebotomy.

Ventose: in the Republican calendar, the month of wind.

venue: place at which an action is tried.

verbatim: (*Lat.*) word for word.

verbatim et literatim: (*Lat.*) word for word and letter for letter.

vermifuge: serving to expel worms and other parasites from the intestinal tract.

verser: a versifier; poet.

vert: in heraldry, the color green.

vestry: an administrative group created within a parish to handle civil duties which included the collection of tithes and other funds to meet civil and religious expenses of the parish, the processioning of land boundaries to prevent disputes, the

employment and sustenance of a minister, the erection and maintenance of the parish buildings (chapel, church, work house, etc.), the appointment of clerks, sextons, processioners, procession masters, etc., and the cars of the poor.

veteran donation: a land grant given by Texas to all veterans who served Texas during the Texas Revolution and were poor, or to a veteran's widow who did not remarry.

vetula: (*Lat.*) little old woman.

vetulus: (*Lat.*) little old man.

vetus: (*Lat.*) aged; old.

viator: (*Lat.*) traveler; a messenger for the magistrates service.

vicarage: the office, duties or residence of a vicar.

victualler: [*also* vicualer] a grocer.

viculus: (*Lat.*); village; hamlet.

videlicet (*Lat.*) namely; to wit; that is to say.

videus: (*Lat.*) living; true to life; vigorous.

vidua: (*Lat.*) widow.

viduus: (*Lat.*) widower; widow.

villanage: [*also* villeinage] base servitude; tenure on condition of doing the lowest kind of services for the lord.

villein: serf.

villeinage: *see* villanage.

villein socage: *see* socage.

villicus: (*Lat.*) steward; overseer of an estate; bailiff.

villita: a small Spanish or Mexican community.

vintager: one who gathers grapes; a winemaker.

vinter: a vintner.

vintner: a wine merchant.

Viper's Dance: *see* St. Vitus' dance.

vir: (*Lat.*) [*also* viri] man; boy; male; husband; soldier.

virgate: an English land measurement equaling one-fourth acre or sometimes one-fourth carcute (thirty acres).

virgin: [*also* virgo] in bonds or licenses of England, an unmarried woman.

Virginia Company of London: a group consisting of Sir Thomas Dale and associates, incorporated as the Virginia Company of London, and granted a charter in 1606 by King James I which entitled them to settle lands in the New World.

Virginia Military District of Ohio: an area set aside in Ohio and granted to men who served during the Revolution under the Commonwealth of Virginia.

virgo: *see* virgin.

viri: *see* vir.

viscount: an officer who acted for the count; sheriff; a peer who was ranked below an earl and above a baron.

vitious intromission: the unwarranted dealing with the movable estate of a deceased person.

viscount: an officer who acted for the count; sheriff; a peer who was ranked below an earl and above a baron.

vitious intromission: the unwarranted dealing with the movable estate of a deceased person.

vivus: (*Lat.*) alive; living; natural.

vixit annos: (*Lat.*) he or she lived (a certain number) years.

vixor: (*Lat.*) wife.

volvulus: in pathology, a twisting of the intestine producing obstruction to, and strangulation of, the part involved.

WXYZ

wad: line or rank; in surveying, the term denoted the lining up of stakes.

wadset: an ancient tenure or lease of land in the Highlands of Scotland similar to a mortgage.

waferer: one who made and sold wafers or thin unleavened cakes.

wafter: a ship which carried passengers and was armed and part of a convoy.

wagoner: a driver of a wagon; a carter.

wain: a cart or wagon.

wainbote: an allowance of timber given to a tenant for the repairs of his wains or wagons.

wain house: a shed for wagons and carts.

wainwright: one who built or repaired wagons.

waiver: an intentional and voluntary giving up of one's rights.

walker: 1: a cloth-worker. 2: in English forest law, an officer who inspected a certain area.

wanter: 1: an unmarried person seeking a spouse. 2: a mole-catcher.

wapentake: a division corresponding to a hundred and a ward in some English counties; the name of a court in such a division or the bailiff serving this court.

warning out: the practice of ordering poor or indigent persons or families to leave a community if they are looked upon as potentially becoming dependent upon the town, township, city, etc., for support.

warp frame: a frame used in making warp lace.

warping bat: a tool used by a wool worker.

warping hook: in rope making, a hook used to hang the yarn on, when warping into hauls.

Warrior's Path: a colonial highway running between Virginia and Kentucky, and later known as the Wilderness Road of Daniel Boone.

washman: a person who applies the wash (or coating) of tin when making tinplate.

wasting: "destructive to health or vigor, as a disease; wasting palsy; progressive muscular atrophy."—*Webster's*

watch care: the temporary receiving into church membership of a new family pending receipt of a letter from the former church.

watchman: one whose job it was to guard the streets at night.

water leader: a person who carts water for sale.

wattle hurdle: a fence made by weaving twigs or branches between sticks.

webber: a weaver.

webster: a weaver.

weddinger: a wedding guest.

Weekly Meeting: a religious gathering of the Society of Friends.

weeper: a badge of mourning such as an arm band or a widow's veil; a professional mourner.

weir: a brushwood fence set up in a stream to trap fish.

well-sweep: a device consisting of a bucket fastened to the end of a pivoted and counterweighted pole used to raise water from a well.

welt: in heraldry, a narrow border added to an ordinary or charge.

Western Reserve: [*also* New Connecticut] a large tract of land located in northeastern Ohio running from the Pennsylvania line to west of Sandusky on the south shore of Lake Erie which was reserved by Connecticut for its own settlers when it ceded its waste lands in 1786.

wey: an English weight that varied with different commodities— a wey of wool is six and one-half tons, or 182 pounds; of oats and barley, 48 bushels; of cheese, 224 pounds; of salt, 40 bushels.

whacker: one who drives a team of oxen, horses, etc.; a very large home.

whang: leather string or a thong.

wharfinger: the person who owned or managed a wharf.

wheelwright: a person who repairs and makes wheels and wheeled vehicles.

whiparse: a schoolmaster.

whiskey: *see* timwhiskey.

whitear: a cleanser of hides.

white house: a dairy.

white rent: 1: blackmail. 2: rent to be paid in silver.

white smith: a maker of utensils in tin, especially dairy utensils.

white tawer: a saddler, harness-maker.

whitewing: a street sweeper.

white woman: a "female" ingredient in alchemy.

whitlow: *see* ancome.

Whitsunday: the seventh Sunday (fiftieth day) after Easter.

whittawer: a saddler.

whooping cough: [*also* pertussis; tussis convulsiva; keuchhusten] a disease characterized by a convulsive cough, and infecting the mucous membrane of the respiratory system.

widow's election: the widow's right to agree or disagree with the husband's will and ask the courts to provide for her in the manner agreed to by the law.

wiffletree: *see* single tree.

wifman: woman.

wildcat bank: a bank that was not given authority to organize by a governing body.

Wilderness Road: *see* Boone's Trace.

willow: 1: a machine with revolving spikes used for cleaning cotton or wool. 2: figuratively, an emblem of sorrow, as to wear the willow which means to mourn.

winding sheet: 1: a shroud. 2: the drippings of wax, sheetlike in form, from a burning candle (an omen of death).

window peeper: the local tax assessor.

window tax: a tax begun in 1696 in England, which increased with the number of windows in one's house.

winnowing: to blow the chaff from grain by wind or a forced current of air.

winter fever: pneumonia.

wisewoman: 1: a midwife. **2:** one having knowledge of black magic.

wissere: teacher; director.

witness corner: [*also* witness tree] a surveyor's mark such as a tree or rock on which is carved a reference, plus the initials w.c. (witness corner) at the corner of a tract of land.

Wolf Scalp Certificate: (1810-15) the bounty claims made for wolves killed and pelts delivered in the Connecticut Western Reserve in Ohio.

Women Friends Petition: (1659) the list of Women Friends Petitioners against tithes submitted to the English Parliament in protesting increased taxes (tithes).

Work Projects Administration: *see* Works Progress Administration.

Works Progress Administration: an agency set up by the Roosevelt administration (1936-43) to counteract the effects of the Great Depression by employing people in government-created jobs—the Historical Records Survey was a project administered by this agency which employed upwards of 3000 clerical personnel to produce inventories of state and local record archives.

worm fence: a zigzag fence of rails; a snake fence.

worm fit: infantile convulsions, usually a reflex action associated with teething, worms, rickets, fever, or diarrhea.

worms: any of the various ailments caused by the working of a worm or resulting in a worm-shaped tumor or growth.

wright: a constructor (e.g., wheelwright, shipwright, etc.).

writ of arrest: *see* writ of capias.

writ of attachment: a court order to a court official to seize and hold property enough to cover debts and court costs for not appearing in court.

writ of capias: [*also* capias; writ of arrest; warrant] a formal arrest document.

writ of capias ad satisfaciendum: [*abbrev.* ca. sa.] a document which required the loser (debtor) to be imprisoned until the debt was paid.

writ of fieri facias: a court order to seize (attach) and sell goods belonging to the loser in a court case to pay debts owed.

writ of summons: a document commanding a person to appear in court.

writ of venire facias: a document issued to call men to be jurors.

Wyandot: *see* Huron.

yard land: land area which varies from fifteen to forty acres, depending on the locality.

yardman: one who works in the yard, especially a railroad yard.

year's provisions: [*also* year's support] a widow is entitled to a twelve months supply of goods and money or provisions out of her husbands estate—this specified amount cannot be used or given to creditors to clear her husband's debts.

yeman: yeoman.

yeme: to take care of; to protect.

yeoman: a freeholder who works his own small estate; an attendant in a royal household; a rank below that of gentlemen.

yeomanette: in World War I, a woman serving in the naval reserve force of the United States the official designation of which is "Yeoman (F)."

York Shilling: *see* eleven-penny bit.

zax: a tool used for trimming slates used in roofing.

Zouaves: a body of light infantrymen in the French army who were distinguished for their physique and dash and the oriental uniform.

Abbrev.

A: in the early colonies, those found guilty of adultery were made to wear the capital letter cut from red cloth and sewn on the outside of their clothing; Academy; Alberta (Canada); America; American.

a: age; about; acre; ante; annus.

AA: Associate in/of Arts.

AAAL: American Academy of Arts and Letters.

AAC: Anno Ante Christum.

A.A.G.: Assistant Adjutant-General.

a.a.r.: against all risks.

AASLH: American Association for State and Local History, Nashville, Tennessee.

AASP: American Antiquarian Society Proceedings.

ab.: about; abbey.

A&HA CO.: Ancient and Honorable Artillery Co.

abbr.: abbreviation.

abd.: abdicated.

Abp.: Archbishop.

abr.: abridged; abridgment.

abs., abstr.: abstract.

ABS: American Bible Society.

abs. re.: absente reo.

abt.: about.

AC: Ante Christum; ancestor chart.

a.c.: attested copy; account current.

ac.: account.

acad.: academy.

ACC: American Computing Centers.

acc.: account; accompanied; according.

ackd.: acknowledged.

actg.: acting.

AD: Anno Domini.

a.d.: ante diem.

Ad.: Archdeaconry.

ADC: Aide-de-Camp.

adcon.: archdeacon; archdeaconry.

add.: addatur; adde.

add. mss.: additional manuscripts.

adj.: adjutant; adjoining; adjourned.

ad loc.: ad locum.

adm.: administrator, administrative.

admin.: administrator; administrative.

Admon.: letters of administration.

admr.: administration.

A.D.S.: autographed document signed.

adv.: adversus.

ae.: aetatis.

aet.: aetatis.

af.: affidavit.

AFAM: Ancient Free and Accepted Masons.

afft.: affidavit.

AFRA: American Family Records Association.

afsd.: aforesaid.

aft.: after; afternoon.

AG: Adjutant General; Accredited Genealogist.

AGBI: *American Genealogical-Biographical Index.*

AGO: Adjutant General's Office.

AHA: American Historical Association.

a.h.l.: ad hunc locum.

a.h.s.: anno humanae solutis.

a.h.v.: (*Lat.*) ad hanc vocem.

AIS: Accelerated Indexing Systems.

AISI: Accelerated Indexing Systems International.

AJHSQ: American Jewish Historical Society Quarterly.

a.k.a.: also known as.

AL: American Legion.

a.l.: signed or autographed letter.

ALA: American Library Association.

ald.: alderman.

alleg.: allegiance.

ALMA: Adoptee's Liberty Movement Association.

a.l.s.: autographed letter signed.

als.: alias.

AME: African Methodist Episcopal Church.

an.: annus; anno.

anc.: ancestry; ancestor; ancient.

An. Do.: Anno Domini.

An. Dom.: Anno Domini.

Angl.: Anglican; Anglicized.

annot.: annotated.

ano.: another; annus.

anon.: anonymous.

ant.: antiquary; antonym.

antiq.: antiquary; antiquities; antiquity; antiquarian.

a.o.: account of.

AOP: American Order of Pioneers.

APG: Association of Professional Genealogists.

APJI: Association for Protection of Jewish Immigrants.

app.: apprentice; approximately; appendix; appointed.

App. Div.: Appellate Division.

appr.: appraisement.

apprd.: apprised; appeared.

approx.: approximately.

apptd.: appointed.

appx.: appendix.

APS: American Philosophical Society.

AR: Anno Regni.

arr.: arrived.

ARR: Anno Regina Regis.

ASG: American Society of Genealogists.

asgd.: assigned.

asr.: assessor.

assn.: association.

asso.: associated; associate.

assoc.: association.

atty: attorney.

au.: gold.

aud.: auditor.

a.v.: annos vixit; ad valorem.

a.w.c.: admon. (letters of administration) with will and codicil annexed.

AWOL: absent without leave.

b.: born; bondsman; banns; book; birth; bachelor; brother; a person convicted of burglary would have a "b" branded on his cheek; a person guilty of blasphemy would have a "B" sewn on his outer clothing..

ba.: bachelor; baptized

bach.: bachelor.

bachr.: bachelor.

BAE: Bureau of American Ethnology, a government agency which published a series of volumes about the culture and characteristics of the American Indians.

bap.: baptized, baptize.

Bart.: Baronet.

batch.: bachelor.

B.B.: Bail Bond.

B.C.: Ball Court; British Columbia; before Christ.

bcer.: birth certificate.

BCG: Board for Certification of Genealogists.

b.d.: birth date.

bd.: bound; buried.

bdt.: birth date.

bef.: before.

bet.: between.

BGL: Branch Genealogical Library of the Church of Jesus Christ of Latter-day Saints.

BIA: Bureau of Indian Affairs.

B.I.C.: born in the covenant.

bil.: brother-in-law.

biog.: biography.

bish.: bishop.

bks.: books, barracks.

bl.: bibliography.

BLM: Bureau of Land Management.

BLW: Bounty Land Warrant.

B.M.: Bench Mark; British Museum.

bndsmn.: bondsman.

bo.: born; bought; bottom.

b.o.t.p.: both of this parish.

bp.: baptized; birthplace.

bpl.: birthplace.

BPOE: Benevolent Protective Order of Elks.

bpt.: baptized.

b.q.: bene quiescat.

Br.: British.

br.: brother.

bro.: brother.

bro-i-l.: brother-in-law.

bro-il.: brother-in-law.

B.S.: in court records, Bill of Sale.

B.T.: Bishop's Transcripts.

Bt.: Baronet.

bu.: buried.

bur.: buried.

c.: cousin; circa; codicil.

C: Roman numeral, 100.

ca.: circa.

CALLS: Certified American Indian Lineage Specialist.

CALS: Certified American Lineage Specialist.

"C and XC": a sub-series designation given to Civil War Pension Application Files as a part of the Civil War and Later Series which included all types of claims filed between 1861 and 1934 and are based on service (1817-1934) excluding World War I service.

capt.: captain.

CAR: National Society, Children of the American Revolution.

ca. sa.: writ of capias ad satisfaciendum.

cath.: cathedral.

cathed.: cathedral.

CC: county clerk, county court, county commissioner, company commander.

CCC: Copyright Clearance Center.

CCP: Court of Common Pleas.

CDA: Colonial Dames of America.

CDIB: Certified Degree of Indian Blood.

CE: Caveat Emptor; Christian Era.

cem.: cemetery.

cen.: census.

cens.: census.

cent.: century.

cer.: certificate.

cf.: confer.

CFI: Computer File Index.

CG: Certified Genealogist.

CGRS: Certified Genealogical Record Searcher.

CH: Court House; Custom House.

ch.: chief; chaplain; children; church; child.

chan.: chancery.

chldn.: children.

chn.: children.

ch/o.: child of.

chr.: christened.

chris.: christened.

CIG: Computer Interest Group.

cir.: circa; circum.

circ.: circa; circum.

CIS: Congressional Information Service.

civ.: civil.

CJ: County Judge.

clk.: clerk.

CO: commanding officer; Colonial Office.

co.: county; company.

cod.: codicil.

C of A: Coat of Arms.

co.h.: coheir, coheiress.

col.: colony.

coil.: college; collections.

com.: comitatus; commissioner; commander; commentary; committee; common; commoner; communicate.

comm.: commissioners.

comp.: company; compiled.

con.: country; conjunx.

con. for.: confessed fornicator.

cons.: consistory.

cont.: continued; contract.

contr.: contraction; contrast; contract.

couns: counsellor.

Court of P's and Q's: Court of Common Pleas and Quarter Sessions.

cous.: cousins.

cous-i-l: cousin-in-law.

CP: Catholic Priest; Court of Common Pleas; Circuit Preacher; Cape of Good Hope, known as Cape Province.

CPC: Canterbury Prerogative Court, London.

c.r.: church report.

CRA: Church Records Archives.

crspd.: correspond; correspondence.

c.s.: copy signed.

CSA: Confederate States of America.

csn.: cousin, cousins.

ct.: court; citation; county.

CTA: cum testamento annexo.

cv.: caveat.

DAB: Dictionary of American Biography.

DAC: National Society of the Daughters of the American Colonists.

DAR: Daughters of the American Revolution.

dau.: daughter.

daugr.: daughter.

dau-i-l.: daughter-in-law.

daus.: daughters.

DAV: Disabled American Veterans.

CW: Civil War; church warden.

DB: Domesday Book.

CZ: territory of Canal Zone.

D: Roman numeral, 500; Dominus (Lord); the letter "D" in colonial New England stood for drunkard and was stitched to the persons outer clothing.

d.: died; decessit (died); dies (day).

DA: District Attorney.

da.: daughter; day.

d.b.n.: de bonis non.

d.b.n.c.t.a.: de bonis non cum testo annexo.

DC: District of Columbia, Deputy Clerk, Deputy County Clerk.

D & C: Dean and Chapter.

DCC: Descendants of Colonial Clergy; Dictionary Card Catalog.

DCG: Descendants of Colonial Governors.

DCHS: Dutchess County Historical Society (New York).

d.&coh.: daughter and coheiress.

d'd.: deceased.

dea.: deacon.

deac.: deacon.

dec.: deceased.

dec'd.: deceased.

dep.: deputy; depot.

dept.: department.

desc.: descendant.

DFPA: Daughters of Founders and Patriots of America.

dft.: defendant.

d.& h.: daughter and heiress.

DHD: Daughters of Holland Dames.

dil.: daughter-in-law.

dio.: diocese.

dis.: discharge.

dist.: district.

div.: division; divinity; divorced.

D.N.: Dominus Noster (Latin) Our Lord.

DNB: Dictionary of National Biography.

d/o: daughter of.

do.: ditto.

doc.: doctor; document.

dom.: domestic.

dpl.: death place.

DR: Daughters of the Revolution; Diocesan Registry.

dr.: doctor; dram.

d.s.: document signed; died single.

dsct.: descendant.

d.s.p.: descessit sine parole.

d.s.p.m.: descessit sine parole mascula.

dt.: date.

dt.: date.

dto.: ditto.

dtr.: daughter.

dt's: delirium tremens.

dum.: died unmarried.

d.um.: died unmarried.

DUVCW: Daughters of the Union Veterans of the Civil War.

DVM: Doctor of Veterinary Medicine.

d.v.m.: decessit vita matris.

d.v.p.: decessit vite partia.

DVR: Society of the Descendants of Washington's Army at Valley Forge.

dwt.: pennyweights.

d.y.: died young.

E.: East or Eastern.

ead.: eadem.

ecux.: a female executor.

E.D.: Enumeration District.

ed.: edited; edition; editor.

educ.: education; educated.

e.g.: exempli gratia.

EIC: East India Company.

ej.: ejus.

eno.: enough.

Ens.: Ensign.

ERIC: Educational Resources Information Center.

est.: estate; established.

estd.: estimated.

etc.: et cetera, and so forth.

et seq.: et sequentes; et sequentia.

et seqq.: et sequentes; et sequentia.

et ux.: et uxor.

et vir.: and husband.

Ev.: Evangelical.

Evang.: Evangelical.

exc.: except; excellency; excepted; exchange.

exec.: executor.

exor.: executor.

exors.: executors.

exox.: executrix.

exr.: executor.

exrx.: excutrix.

exs.: executors.

extm.: ex testamento.

exx.: executrix.

f.: folio; father; female; feast; feet; farm; following.

fa.: father; facias.

F.A.: Field Artillery.

F&AM: Free and Accepted Masons.

fam.: family; families.

FARC: Federal Archives and Records Centers (branches of the National Archives).

FAS.: Free African Society

FASG.: Fellow American Society of Genealogists.

father-i-l: father-in-law.

F.B.: Family Bible.

f.e.: for example.

ff.: fecerunt; following (pages); *(Old English)* capital F.

FF's: First Families.

FFV: First Families of Virginia.

FGRA: Family Group Record Archives.

FGS: Federation of Genealogical Societies.

fi.: fieri.

fil.: father-in-law.

f. inl.: father-in-law.

FISG: Fellow Institute of American Genealogy (defunct)

fl.: florit

FLT: Friendship, Love, Truth—an inscription used on cemetery stones.

f.m.: free mulatto.

f.n.: free negro.

FR: Family Registry.

FSG: Fellow, Society of Genealogists (London).

ft.: foot; fort.

g.: grand; great.

GAR: Grand Army of the Republic.

G.B.: Great Britain.

gch: grandchildren.

gdn.: guardian.

GH: *Genealogical Helper.*

GLC: Genealogical Library Catalog.

GLO: General Land Office.

gm.: grandmother.

GMRV: Granite Mountain Records Vault.

godf.: godfather.

godm.: godmother.

gp.: grandparents.

GPAI: *Genealogical Periodical Annual Index.*

g.r.: grave record.

grd.: guardian.

grdn.: guardian.

gr/d/o: granddaughter of.

grf.: grandfather.

grm.: grandmother.

gr/s/o: grandson of.

g.s.: grave stone.

GS: Genealogical Society of Utah.

GSW 1812: General Society of the War of 1812.

Gt. Br.: Great Britain.

gt. gr.: great grand.

GTT: Gone to Texas.

gu.: gules.

l/h, 2/h: first husband, second husband, etc.

h.: husband; heir; heiress.

HCA: High Court of Admiralty.

hdqrs.: headquarters.

HEIC: Honourable East India Company.

her.: heraldry.

hers.: herself.

HIAS: Hebres Immigrant Aid Society.

HJS: Hic Jacet Sepultus.

HLS: Hic Loco Situs.

HM: His or Her Majesty.

h.m.: hoc mense.

HMS: Her (or His) Majesty's Service or Ship.

hon.: honorable; honor; honorary.

hon. dis.: honorably discharged.

HRIP: Hic Requiescit in Pac.

HS: Holland Society.

HSA: Huguenot Society of America.

h.t.: hoc tempore.

hund.: hundred.

hus.: husband.

I: in New England persons who had committed the crime of incest were required to wear the letter "I" sewn to their outer clothing.

ibid.: ibidem.

IDN: In Dei Nomie.

i.e.: id est.

i.f.: ipse fecit.

IGI: International Genealogical Index.

ign.: ignorant; ignotus.

i.h.: iacet hic.

I.H.S.: first 3 letters of Greek name for Jews, a symbol of the Holy Name.

illus: illustrated.

imp.: importation.

inc.: incorporated; incomplete.

incl.: included; inclusive.

incl.: included; inclusive.

I.N.D.: In Nomine Die.

IND.S.C.: Indian Survivors' Certificates.

IND.S.O.: Indian Survivors' Originals.

Ind.T.: Indian Territory.

Ind.Ter.: Indian Territory.

Ind.W.C.: Indian Widow's Certificate.

Ind.W.O.: Indian Widows' Originals.

ined.: ineditus.

inf.: infantry; infant; informed.

info.: information.

inh.: inherited.

inhab.: inhabited.

in loc. cit.: loco citata.

inq.: inquiry.

I.N.R.I.: Jesus Nazarenus Rex Judaeorum.

ins.: insert.

INS: Immigration and Naturalization Service.

inst.: institute; institution.

int.: intentions; interested; interred.

inv.: inventory.

invt.: inventory.

IOOF: Independent Order of Odd Fellows.

i.p.m.: inquisitione post mortem.

i.q.: iden quod.

JA: Judge Advocate.

JNH: Journal of Negro History.

JP: Justice of the Peace.

JPS: Jewish Publication Society.

Jr.: Junior.

jud.: judicial.

judic.: judicious.

junr.: junior.

jut.: jurat.

jur.: jurat.

juv.: juvenis.

k.: killed; king.

kn.: known.

knt.: knight.

kt.: knight.

l.: license; law.

L: Latin; Liber.

labr.: laborer.

Lat.: Latin.

lb.: libra, or pound.

LBC: Letter Book Copy.

LC: Library of Congress.

lnd.: land.

ldr.: leader.

LDS: The Church of Jesus Christ of Latter-day Saints.

l.e.: local elder in a church.

letters C.T.A.: letters cum testamento annexed.

li.: lived; living.

lib.: liber; library.

lie.: license.

liv.: lived, living.

liv. abt.: lived about.

l.l.: loco ladato.

ll.: lines.

lnd.: land.

loc.cit.: loco citato.

l.p.: local preacher.

l.s.: locus sigilli.

ltd.: limited.

m.: month; male; married; mother; maritus.

m/l, m/2: married first, married second, etc.

mag.: magistrate.

mat.: maternal.

m.bn.: marriage banns.

MCA: Microfilm Corporation of America.

MCC: Microfilm Card Catalog.

MCD: Municipal Civil District.

MD: Doctor of Medicine; Middle Dutch.

md.: married.

mem.: member; membership; memorials; memoir.

ment.: mentioned.

messrs.: plural of mister.

Mex. S.C.: Mexican Survivors' Certificates.

Mex. S.O.: Mexican Survivors' Originals.

Mex. W.C.: Mexican Widows' Certificate.

Mex. W.O.: Mexican Widows' Originals.

MG: Minister of the Gospel.

m.h.: meeting house.

MHG: Middle High German.

m.i.: monumental inscription.

mi.: mile, miles.

MIA: Missing in Action.

mil.: military; militia; mother-in-law.

milit.: military.

min.: minister; minor; minutes.

m-in-l.: mother-in-law.

MLG: Middle Low German.

MLW: Military Land Warrant.

mm.: matrimonium.

MM: abbreviation for Monthly Meeting of Society of Friends (Quakers).

m.o.: mustered out.

mo.: month; mother.

Mons.: Monsignor.

morg.: morgen.

mors.: death; corpse.

mov.: moved.

MQ: *Mayflower Quarterly.*

Mr.: Mister.

Mrs.: Mistress.

ms.: manuscript.

mss.: manuscripts.

mtg.: meeting; mortgage.

mvd.: moved.

my/d: my daughter.

N.: Negro; North.

n.: natus, nephew, nomen; nupta; name.

NA: National Archives in Washington, D.C.

na.: naturalized.

NARS: National Archives and Record Service.

nat.: natus.

NCO: non-commissioned officer.

NCPC: National Personnel Records Center, Civilian Personnel Records.

n.d.: no date.

N.E.: North East; New England.

NEH: National Endowment for the Humanities.

NEHGS: New England Historic Genealogical Society.

neph.: nephew.

neph-i-l: nephew-in-law.

nfi: no further information.

nfk: nothing further known.

NGS: National Genealogical Society.

NGSCIG: National Genealogical Society Computer Interest Group.

NGSQ: *National Genealogical Society Quarterly.*

NHPRC: National Historical Publications and Records Commission.

rim.: name.

nmed.: named.

nms.: names.

not.: noted.

NP: Notary Public.

n.p.: no place.

nr.: none recorded; not recorded; naturalized.

NS: New Style calendar; Nova Scotia.

NSC: Navy Survivors' Certificates.

NSCDA: National Society of the Colonial Dames of America.

NSDAR: National Society, Daughter of the American Revolution.

NSO: Navy Survivor's Originals.

NUCMC: *National Union Catalog of Manuscript Collections.*

nunc.: nuncupative.

N.W.: North West.

NWC: Navy Widow's Certificates.

NWO: Navy Widows' Originals.

NW. Terr.: North West Territory.

n.x.n.: no christian name.

NYGBR: *New York Genealogical and Biographical Record; New York Genealogical and Biographical Register.*

o.: oath; optimus.

O.B.: Order Book.

ob.: obit; obiit; obiter.

ob. caelebs: obit caelebs.

obit.: obituary.

ob.s.p.: obiit sine prole.

ob.s.p.m.: obiit sine prole masulus.

obt.: obiit.

ob. unm.: obit unmarried.

ob.v.p.: obiit vita patris.

o.c.: only child; opere citato.

OCLC: Online Computer Library Center, Inc., in Dublin, Ohio.

OE: Old English.

OED: *Oxford English Diction*ary.

off.: official.

offi.: official.

oft.: often.

OM: Organized Militia.

o.p.: out of print.

op.cit.: opere citato.

ord.: ordinance; order; ordained; ordinary.

org.: organization.

orig.: origin; original.

OS: Old Style calendar.

o.s.p.: obiit sine prole.

o.t.p.: of this parish.

p.: page; pater; per; populus; parentage; parents; pence.

p.a.: power of attorney.

pam.: pamphlet.

pamph.: pamphlet.

par.: parish; parent; parents.

pat.: patent; patented; paternal.

PCC: Prerogative Court of Canterbury.

pchd.: purchased.

PCY: Prerogative Court of York.

PE: Presiding Elder.

perh.: perhaps.

petitn., petn.: petition.

petr.: petitioner.

ph.: parish.

PI: Preliminary inventories.

pion.: pioneer.

PJP: Probate Judge of the Peace.

PLB: Poor Law Board.

pit.: plaintiff.

P.M.: Post Meridiem, afternoon; Post Mortem, after death; Police Magistrate.

P.O.: Post Office.

POA: Power of Attorney.

POE: Port of Entry.

pp.: pages; patres.

PPA: per power of attorney.

pp.: pages; patres.

PPA: per power of attorney.

pr.: proved; probated.

p.r.: parish register.

prec., precd.: preceding.

PRO: Public Record Office.

pro.: province; probated; proved.

prob.: probated; probably.

prop.: property.

propr.: proprietor.

PRS: Pedigree Referral Service.

pt.: point; port; petition; pint.

ptf.: plaintiff.

pub.: published; public; publisher; publication.

pvt.: private.

pymt.: payment.

q.: quarto, oversized book.

q.e.: quod est.

q.q.v.: quae vide.

q.v.: quod vide.

q.y.: query.

r.: rector; regins; rex; rejected; river; road.

R.: Range; Rabbi; River; Road.

rat.: rated.

R.C.: Roman Catholic.

rcdr.: recorder.

rcpt.: receipt.

RD: release of dower rights.

re.: regarding.

reg.: register.

Reg. Gen.: Registrar General.

rel.: relative; religion; released.

reid.: relieved.

rel-i-l: relative-in-law.

ren.: renunciation.

rep.: report; representative; reprint; reprinted.

repl.: replaced; replacement.

repud.: repudiate.

res.: research; residence; resides.

ret.: retired.

Rev.: Reverend; Revolutionary War.

Rev. War: Revolutionary War.

RG: Registered Genealogist.

rgstr.: registrar.

RIP: requiescat in pace; rest in peace.

RLDS: Reorganized Church of Jesus Christ of Latter-day Saints.

rlnq.: relinquished.

Rom.: Roman.

RR: Railroad.

RW: Revolutionary War.

S.: south; section.

s.: soldier; survivor; son; sepultus; spinster; sons; successor; shilling.

s.a.: secundum artem; sine anno.

s and coh.: son and coheir.

s and h.: son and heir.

SAR: Sons of the American Revolution.

SASE: self-addressed stamped envelope.

SC: Society of the Cincinnati; Schomburg Center for Research in Black Culture; Survivors Certificates.

SCV: Sons of Confederate Veterans.

SCW: Society of Colonial Wars.

s'd: said—found in legal documents.

SDA: Seventh Day Adventists.

S.E.: South East.

sec.: second; secretary; section; sector; security.

seqq.: sequentia.

ser.: servant; service,

serv.: servant; service.

settl.: settled; settler; settlement.

sev.: several.

sh.: share; ship.

s.& h.: son and heir.

sil: son-in-law.

sin.: sine.

sis.: sister.

sis-i-l: sister-in-law.

sis-il: sister-in-law.

SJ: Society of Jesus.

s.l: sine loco.

s.l.p.: sine legitima prole.

sn.: sine.

s/o: son of.

SO: Survivors' Originals.

soc.: society; societies.

s.p.: sine prole.

SPG: Society for the Propagation of the Gospel.

s.p.l.: sine prole legitima.

s.p.m.: sine prole mascula.

spr.: sponsor; spinster.

s.p.s.: sine prole supersite.

sr.: senior; soror.

srnms.: surnames.

ss.: supra scriptum.

st.: saint, street.

sup: supply; superior.

supt.: superintendent.

surg.: surgeon.

SUV: Sons of Union Veterans.

SV: Sons of Veterans.

sw.: swear; swore.

T.: Township.

t.: tomus; tempore.

temp.: tempore.

terr.: territory.

test.: testament.

tho.: though.

thot.: thought.

thro.: through.

TIB: Temple (Records) Index Bureau.

tn.: town; township.

top.: topographical.

Tp.: Township.

t.p.: title page.

t.p.m.: title page mutilated.

t.p.w.: title page wanting.

tr.: troop; translated; translation.

transc.: transcribed.

transl.: translation.

treas.: treasurer.

TRIB: Temple Records Index Bureau.

TVA: Tennessee Valley Authority.

twn.: town.

twp.: township.

ty.: territory.

u.d.: ultimo die.

UDC: United Daughters of the Confederacy.

UGS: Utah Genealogical Society of the Church of Jesus Christ of Latter-day Saints.

U.K.: United Kingdom.

ult.: ultimo.

lto.: ultimo.

unasgd.: unassigned.

unc.: uncle.

unk.: unknown.

unm.: unmarried.

unorg: unorganized.

USCG: United States Coast Guard.

USCT: United States Colored Troops.

USMC: United States Marine Corps.

USN: United States Navy.

USWPA: United States Works Progress Administration.

v.a.: vixit annos.

var.: variation; various; variant.

VDM: Verbi Dei Minister; Voluns Dei Minister.

VFW: Veterans of Foreign Wars.

VIP: Very Important Person.

Vie.: Viscount; Viscountess.

Visc.: Viscount; Viscountess.

Visct.: Viscount; Viscountess.

vit.: vital.

viz.: videlicet.

V.L: Vulgar Latin.

v.m.: vita matris.

vols.: volunteers; volumes.

v.p.: vita patris.

v.r.: vital records.

vs.: versus.

v.s.: vital statistics.

w.: west; will; wife; widow.

wag.: wagoner.

W.B.: Will Book.

WD: War Department.

w.d.: will dated.

wd.: widow; ward.

wf./o: wife of.

wh.: which; who.

wit.: witness.

wk.: week; work.

wnt.: wants.

WO: Widow's Originals.

w/o: wife of.

W.O.: Warrant Officer.

w.p.: will probated; will proved.

WPA: Works Progress Administration; Work Projects Administration.

WRHS: Western Reserve Historical Society.

W.S.: Writer to the Signet.

wtn.: witness.

ww.: widow.

ww/o: widow of.

wwr.: widower.

X: a mark made by person instead of a signature; Christ; Christian.

XC: *see* C and XC.

x ch.: exchange.

Xn.: Christian.

Xnty: Christianity.

Xped: Christened.

Xr.: Christian.

Xt.: Christ.

Xtian: Christian.

Xty: Christianity.

y.: year.

yd.: graveyard.

yr.: year; younger; your.